CASE STUDIES IN
CULTURAL ANTHROPOLOGY

GENERAL EDITORS
George and Louise Spindler
STANFORD UNIVERSITY

THE CHEYENNES

Indians of the Great Plains

second edition

By

E. ADAMSON HOEBEL

University of Minnesota

HOLT, RINEHART AND WINSTON

NEW YORK   CHICAGO   SAN FRANCISCO   DALLAS
MONTREAL   TORONTO   LONDON   SYDNEY

To Wo-He-Hiv—Morning Star:
"He was the greatest of our chiefs."

Library of Congress Cataloging in Publication Data

Hoebel, Edward Adamson, 1906–
  The Cheyennes.

  (Case studies in cultural anthropology)
  Bibliography: p. 134
  1. Cheyenne Indians. I. Title. II. Series.
E99.C53H6   1978   970'.004'97   77-25471
ISBN 0-03-022686-4

  2 3 4 144 9 8 7 6 5 4

Foreword

About the Series

These case studies in cultural anthropology are designed to bring to students, in beginning and intermediate courses in the social sciences, insights into the richness and complexity of human life as it is lived in different ways and in different places. They are written by men and women who have lived in the societies they write about and who are professionally trained as observers and interpreters of human behavior. The authors are also teachers, and in writing their books they have kept the students who will read them foremost in their minds. It is our belief that when an understanding of ways of life very different from one's own is gained, abstractions and generalizations about social structure, cultural values, subsistence techniques, and the other universal categories of human social behavior become meaningful.

About the Author

E. Adamson Hoebel is Regents Professor Emeritus of Anthropology at the University of Minnesota. He holds the Ph.D. in anthropology from Columbia University. For a number of years, he taught anthropology at New York University and subsequently at the University of Utah, where he was also Dean of the University College (Arts and Sciences). He has served as Fulbright Professor in anthropology at Oxford and in law at Catholic University in Holland. He has done field work among the Northern Cheyenne (1935 and 1936) and among the Comanches (1933), Northern Shoshone (1934), Pueblo Indians of New Mexico (1945–1949), and in West Pakistan (1961). He is the author of *Anthropology, The Political Organization and Law-ways of the Comanche Indians,* and *The Law of Primitive Man.* He is co-author (with Karl N. Llewellyn) of *The Cheyenne Way,* (with Ernest Wallace) of *The Comanches,* and (with E. L. Frost) of *Cultural and Social Anthropology.* Dr. Hoebel is a past-President of the American Ethnological Society and the American Anthropological Association. He has served as a director of the American Council of Learned Societies and the Social Science Research Council, and as a member of the Advisory Panels of the Office of Social Science Research, National Science Foundation, the Behavioral Science Training Program, National Institute of General Medical Sciences, and the United States Arms Control and Disarmament Agency.

About the New Edition

This is a lively book about a high-spirited but self-controlled people who had a complex, satisfying way of life before it was uprooted by the white man. With the help of the Cheyenne elders still living when he did his field work, and through a masterly study of the surviving culture, Dr. Hoebel has made this way of life live again.

A well-rounded picture of the Cheyenne emerges in this case study. They are a people who are not "typical" of anything—the Cheyenne are too unique for that—but they represent much of the Plains Indian way of life that is so much a part of the drama of our West.

Among the people with whom Dr. Hoebel has worked, the Cheyenne stand out as a group who have won his admiration and liking. Their democratic tolerance; the value they place upon individual liberty, balanced by group cooperativeness; their intellectual stamina, balanced with activity; their self-assurance—all of these qualities place the Cheyenne high on a scale of values that we can all appreciate. But the Cheyenne created and maintained these values within a framework of social life very different from our own. A case study of the Cheyenne therefore offers the opportunity of gaining a new perspective on human behavior.

In this new edition, Dr. Hoebel has supplied us with a new first chapter, "The Search for a New Homeland," and two new chapters following the description of the climax culture of the Cheyenne (1800–1850), "War with the United States" and "The New Era." These three new chapters enhance the value of this case study significantly, for they put the "ethnographic present" climax culture into the perspective of time and history.

Whenever we have used this case study in its first edition in introductory anthropology, we have been asked repeatedly, "What happened to the people after the whites came?" and, "What's happening today?" or even, "Why aren't the Cheyenne the way they are described in this case study?" We have also had letters from people who are not students in our classes who want to know why the case study did not describe the Cheyenne as they actually are. The original case study was a superb descriptive interpretation of the climax culture of the Cheyenne, and as such it was widely appreciated—it has long been one of the most widely used case studies in the series. But these are legitimate questions. The new edition answers them.

The tragic events that crowded upon each other after the Civil War in the United States ended with the consignment of the remnants of the Cheyenne people to two reservations. These incidents are only a part of the story, which is handled by Dr. Hoebel with great objectivity. The remainder of the story, told in the last chapter, "The New Era," is about what happened after the reservation period began. It too is tragic, but it is also hopeful. We leave to the reader the discovery of these elements, brought together by Dr. Hoebel with consummate skill.

GEORGE AND LOUISE SPINDLER
General Editors

Phlox, Wisconsin

Contents

Morning Star. Photo by L. A. Huffman, 1879. (Courtesy of E. Adamson Hoebel)

Introduction

The Cheyenne Indians, or *Tsistsistas,* meaning "The People," are one of the most notable of the western tribes who inhabited the Great Plains, the open country lying west of the Mississippi River and east of the Rocky Mountains. They were famous among early travelers for the chastity of their women and the courage of their warriors; in later years, when everything was in change, they were considered the most conservative of the Plains Indians. Their attitudes toward sex and war and toward the maintenance of their social order are the outstanding features of their way of life. These were the main themes of the first edition of this culture case study, which undertook to analyze the reasons for the Cheyenne attitudes, how these attitudes produced a distinctive effect on Cheyenne behavior, and how the Cheyennes worked out a remarkably effective and satisfying society. Our major concern will be to show how prior and present social history, basic cultural premises, psychological traits, physical and biological environment, and social structure all interact to give this culture its characteristic cast as it existed at its high point. This occurred just before the middle of the last century, when the Cheyennes were still a free and independent people—the time which we shall call the Climax: 1800–1850.

When first met by European explorers, the Cheyenne resided in the woodland country of the upper Mississippi Valley, mostly in southeastern Minnesota. Unfriendly neighbors, the Chippewa and Sioux (Dakota), who obtained firearms from the fur traders well before the Cheyenne could lay hands on them, drove the Cheyenne from their homeland and started them on a long, gradual westward movement in search of a new haven. Eventually, they came to rest in the far reaches of the high plains: the northern bands in western Nebraska, eastern Colorado and Wyoming—and, ultimately, on a reservation in southeastern Montana; the southern bands in southwestern Nebraska, western Kansas, southeastern Colorado, eventually ending up on a reservation in western Oklahoma. The southern reservation lasted only twenty-five years, however.

In their westward movement, the Cheyenne, early in the eighteenth century, became closely associated with the sedentary village tribes of the middle Missouri River—namely, the Mandan, Hidatsa, and Arikara. These tribes were old-time gardeners who relied upon hunting for subsidiary subsistence. They lived in permanent villages constructed of large, semisubterranean earth lodges (see Wilson 1934). They were organized into matrilineal clans, and a married couple lived with the bride's parents.

The Cheyenne then built their own earth-lodge villages and cultivated corn, beans, and squash, in the manner of their new neighbors. They also acquired new ceremonial ideas as well as new subsistence techniques. Their way of life was both sedate and sedentary, but was constantly threatened by marauding Sioux or Chippewa war parties.

The use of the riding horse, which had been introduced into the New World by the Spanish conquistadores, had diffused northward and then east to reach the Cheyennes around 1760. New vistas opened for them. The plains offered an escape from the predatory Sioux—and they were teeming with bison and antelope, if only one could conveniently traverse the great dry stretches between the widely scattered waterways with reasonable prospects of locating the herds, and with the means to transport enough meat to the base camp to sustain the tribe through the winter. Where men on foot found such prospects dim, men on horseback found them bright. By 1830, the Cheyennes were sufficiently equipped with horses to have completely abandoned the village life of gardeners for the nomadic life of hunters. Simultaneously, they were adding guns to their hunting and fighting equipage. Mobility and the great prizes to be won in hunt and war transformed much of their culture, but the past—as always—left its imprint.

The Cheyennes, as they are presented in Part Two of this case study, are the Cheyennes of the period 1830–1850, when their adaptation to nomadic horse culture was at flood tide, when white hunters had not yet exterminated the buffalo, nor had settlers preempted their lands, nor had they had a single battle with the military forces of the United States. This part of the book is written in the "ethnographic present," which means that it is presented descriptively in the present tense better to help the reader to get the feel of the culture as lived by the Cheyenne. The last two chapters (which, like the first, are newly written for this edition) should make it abundantly clear that things are not, and have not been for some time, as described for the Climax Period in Part Two.

The addition of the historical materials adds a stronger picture of culture change and adaptation which the Cheyennes have experienced over the past three hundred years. This has been made possible through the recent publication of historical researches by the Plains archaeologist W. R. Wood (1971), cultural anthropologists Jacob Jablow (1950) and F. R. Secoy (1953), and the historians D. J. Berthrong (1963; 1976) and D. Lavender (1954).

The author did extensive field work among the Northern Cheyenne in 1935 and 1936, concentrating on the recording of traditional cases of disputes and dispute-settlement. Old people were still living then who had vivid and well-informed memories of the old days. Fortunately, the Northern Cheyennes were intensively studied at first hand from about 1885 to 1910 by a very acute and sympathetic observer, George Bird Grinnell, whose two-volume work, *The Cheyenne Indians,* is a classic of anthropological research. It was my good fortune to be aided throughout my own Cheyenne field studies by Mr. Grinnell's old interpreter and friend, High Forehead (Willis Rowland). I also had the unstinting friendship and cooperation of a number of elderly Cheyennes. It is on the basis of what I learned from them and the researches of Grinnell that this book primarily rests. It also draws to a lesser extent upon the Cheyenne studies of Fred Eggan, James Mooney, George A. Dorsey, John Stands in Timber and Margot Liberty, and Peter J. Powell. John Moore kindly made unpublished materials on Cheyenne cosmology available to me.

PART ONE

Prelude
(1680–1800)

1 / The search for a new homeland

It was the year 1680. The day was February twenty-fourth. The French trader-explorer, Sieur de La Salle, was at work with his men building a small fort on the banks of Lake Peoria, not far from where Peoria, Illinois, now stands. Their labors were interrupted by the arrival of a party of Indians who told La Salle they had come from their home at the head of the great river (the Mississippi) in search of him. In their country were many beaver and other fur-bearing animals, they said. If only La Salle would come up the river to their villages with them, they would gladly trade many furs for the goods he had to offer.

La Salle wrote that they came from a tribe called *Chaa.*

They had, on their own initiative, traveled more than three hundred miles in hopes of getting access to objects of European manufacture—knives, axes, pots, guns, and articles of personal adornment. Trade was not forced on them, it was eagerly desired for the sake of the material goods it offered. The Chaa in 1680 could not be aware of the consequences that the European fur trade would have for them over the next three hundred years. It would lead them to leave their woodland home in central Minnesota, to migrate southwestward to the prairie lands along the Minnesota River, then northwestward to settle along various tributaries of the Red River of the North, in the Dakotas. Soon thereafter, they would wander farther into the plains, building earth-lodge villages in close proximity to the great villages of the Mandan, Hidatsa, and Arikara—the maize-growing and buffalo-hunting tribes whose ancestors had for several centuries exploited the fertile bottom lands of the middle Missouri river country. Then again, the Chaa would move ever westward, and south, eventually to become horse-mounted nomads, living in hide tipis, embroiled in continuous wars over hunting territories.

Who were these Chaa who sought out La Salle? Most anthropologists and historians of the fur trade believe they were indeed the peoples we now know as Cheyenne. The Dakota Sioux, who also lived in Minnesota, call them *Shahiyena* or *Shahiela,* meaning "people who talk differently"—"foreigners" or "aliens." Other Siouxan-speaking tribes, such as the Arikara and Pawnee, call them *Shar'ha.* A French map, dated 1678, which is based on information supplied by the explorer, Louis Joliet, places the "Chaiena" on the east side of the Mississippi River in southwestern Wisconsin. From one or another variant of the Sioux name with which the French first came in contact, came Cheyenne.

To themselves the Cheyennes were no aliens or speakers of a strange tongue. They know themselves as *Tsistsistas,* "Human Beings," or "The Peo-

4

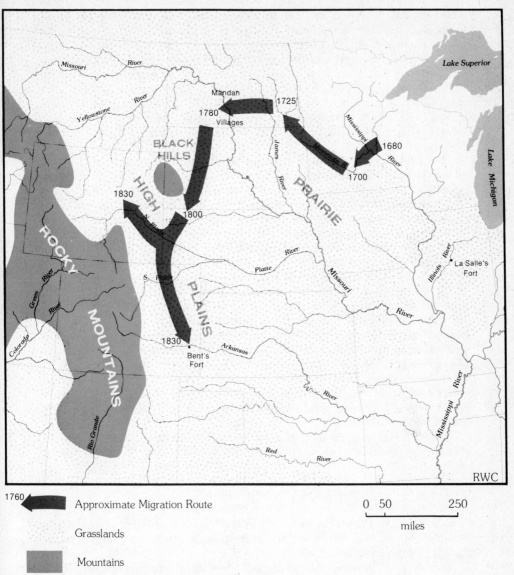

Cheyenne migrations, 1680–1850—a people in search of a homeland.

ple," a common form of elemental ethnocentrism. Their language belongs to the great speech-family known as Algonkin.

THE EASTERN WOODLANDS PHASE

The Cheyennes, at the dawn of historic records for the Great Northwest, as their homeland came to be known, were thus living at the very edge of the ecological area known as the Eastern Woodlands. This area, from the Great Lakes and St. Lawrence River Valley north to the sub-Arctic tundra, was inhabited largely by Algonkin-speakers like themselves. No archaeological sites which can be satisfactorily identified as belonging to the Cheyennes in Minnesota or Wisconsin have as yet been identified. Nor did any of the early historians leave any notes on their tribal lifeways. However, some likely inferences as to their mode of livelihood can be drawn from the known archaeological record of the settlements and food-getting practices of the peoples who inhabited the upper Mississippi Valley around the middle of the seventeenth century.

They probably lived in permanent, small villages on the shores of the lakes which dotted forested countryside. Their houses were built over shallow, excavated floors, above which were raised wooden frames. Each frame was covered with elm or birch bark or earth packed over wattle walls and roof. It is impossible to speculate on how large the early Cheyenne villages may have been, or how many of them there were. But it was not a large tribe, and the likelihood is that not more than two or three hundred people would have made up a good-sized local group, or village.

The basic source of food in the area was wild rice, which grew abundantly in the shallow bays of the lakes and river bottoms. The rice was harvested from birchbark canoes, then hulled, and roasted for storage. Deer, rabbits, and other small game were snared or hunted with bow and arrow, and occasionally forest bison were killed. Ducks and geese were plentiful, and fish were taken in quantities. Although primarily food gatherers and hunters, the Cheyennes probably did some gardening. Summer and fall were periods of bountiful food and benign climate. Winter was a time of difficult survival under conditions of severe cold and deep snow which made hunting difficult and stretched the stored food supplies to their limits. Starvation must have been a frequent threat.

Although war was probably not a large-scale enterprise, it was surely an ever-present possibility, as it was for all American Indians.

THE PRAIRIE PHASE

How long the Cheyennes had lived in the Upper Mississippi region is impossible to say. We do know, however, that by 1690 they began to be dislodged from their homeland.

At first, the Cheyennes moved because they were forced to by the Woodland Sioux and the Assiniboine and Cree, their more numerous and better armed neighbors living to the east and north of them in Minnesota. The Sioux had already had their first contacts with European guns and metal goods around 1650, when they began to meet Hurons and Ottawas who had been driven from the eastern Great Lakes area by the superior military effectiveness of the expanding Iroquois—close allies of the British. The Huron and Ottawa were Algonkin-speaking Indians of the same language family as the Cheyennes.

The Eastern Sioux, who had less direct contact with the sources of European goods than did the Huron and Ottawa, had fewer guns with which to protect themselves. They fell back upon the Cheyennes by moving westward.

The Assiniboine and Cree were at the same time obtaining guns directly from the traders at Hudson Bay. They pressed upon the more poorly armed Cheyennes from the north, and the Cheyennes began to seek security elsewhere.

According to Dakota Sioux traditions, the Cheyennes first reestablished themselves in the prairie country along the Minnesota River in the extreme southwestern part of Minnesota before 1700. They soon found their habitation of this desirable territory untenable under the prevailing conditions of continuous warfare with the Sioux, and one by one abandoned their Minnesota River villages to move northwestward to the Sheyenne River in South Dakota, where by 1725 they are known to have established at least one village of earth-lodges. Within fifty years, an indefinite number of Cheyenne villages had been established along the length of the Sheyenne, which for the most part flows from north to south through low-lying prairies, and only fifty miles west of the great Red River.

The Cheyennes had left their prehistoric woodland base behind and had now entered the Prairie Phase of their changing lifeways.

While it lasted, it must have been a good life. They were in a country which teemed with bison, elk, moose, deer, bear, wolves, raccoons, fox, otter (all edible providers of furs—a double bounty). Wildfowl was available in surplus quantities, as were the game fish so prized by sportsmen today— sturgeon and northern and wall-eyed pike—as well as catfish and others.

From the horticultural Sioux-speaking tribes to the south of them, the Oto and Iowa, the newly located Cheyennes learned improved gardening techniques. And they were only one hundred miles east of the Mandan and Hidatsa, whom I like to call "The Parisians of the Plains," for their sedentary earth-lodge villages were the centers of a thousand-year-old climax of river valley culture adapted to gardening and hunting in the Plains. They were sophisticated people with a rich and dramatic ceremonial life, tanners of fine buffalo robes, growers of surplus stocks of corn and vegetables, and astute traders to whom less richly endowed tribes brought meat and hides to exchange for finished robes and garden produce. The Cheyennes were to learn much from them.

Even as the Cheyennes were establishing themselves on the Sheyenne River, one hundred miles to the east, the French trader, Pierre de La Verendrye, and his two sons reached the Mandan in 1738 to open direct trade with the French post on Lake Winnepeg. When the La Verendrye sons returned to the Mandan the following year, the Mandans had acquired their first horses in trade with a more western tribe, possibly the Crow, who in turn would have got theirs from the Utes and Comanches, who had first started stealing them from the Spanish colonies of Texas and New Mexico some years before.

The European horse, diffusing north from New Spain and then eastward, had finally met with the European gun spreading westward among the tribes from the Great Lakes and southwest from Hudson Bay. Note the date well—1739! The time of the warring, raiding, buffalo and antelope hunting nomads of the Great Plains was at hand. The brief prairie phase of Cheyenne existence was about to close. There would be an overlapping interlude when some Cheyennes would establish themselves in fortified earth-lodge villages between the Mandan and Arikara locations on the Missouri River, but by 1804, when the Lewis and Clark Expedition passed up the river on its way to the Columbia and the Pacific Northwest, even these Cheyenne villages had all been abandoned. The Cheyennes had taken to horses in search of bison and to escape the pestiferous Ojibwa and Sioux—as well as smallpox and measles. They were fully established in the third phase of their historic existence: that of the nomadic hunter-warriors.

The destruction of one Cheyenne village on the Sheyenne River circa 1740 (before the Cheyenne had horses) is detailed by David Thompson, a trader, who wrote in 1800:

> They (the Sheyenne River Cheyennes) were a neutral tribe between the Salteurs (Ojibwa or Chippewa) for many years . . . but the latter suspected they favored the Sioux, a very large party (of Ojibwa) having been once unsuccessful in discovering their enemies (turned on the Cheyennes), destroying their village and murdering most of them. . . . The Shians having been nearly exterminated, abandoned their old territories and fled southward across the Missouri, where they are now a wandering tribe (Coues 1897:I, 144).

At a somewhat later date (circa 1780), another village on the Sheyenne River was destroyed by a carefully organized Chippewa war party, bent on revenge. The story was told by a Chippewa chief, named Sugar.
According to his account:

> Our people and the Chyenne's for several years had been doubtful friends; *but as they had Corn and other Vegetables, we had not and of which we were fond, and traded with them,* (italics added) we passed over and forgot, many things we did not like; *until lately.*

Convinced that the Cheyennes, and not the Sioux, were the killers of some missing Chippewa hunters, the Chippewas gathered a war party of one hundred and fifty fighters which concealed itself for a week near the Cheyenne village. The village was kept under continuous surveillance by two Chippewa scouts hidden in an oak grove growing about a mile from the village. Not wanting to attack a stockaded village on foot across a mile of open prairie, the Chippewas waited patiently for a favorable opportunity. It came when one of the scouts returned one morning to announce that the Cheyennes had rounded up their horses and brought them to the village. About noon, the second scout came in to report that the Cheyennes had left on a hunting expedition and that the village was largely deserted.
Sugar's story continues:

> We now marched leisurely . . . to give the hunting party time to proceed so far as to be beyond the sound of our Guns . . . (finally), as we ran over (the open plain), we were perceived, there were several Horses in the Village on Which the young people got, and rode off.
> We entered the village and put everyone to death, except three Women; after taking every thing we wanted, we quickly set fire to the Village and with all haste retreated for those who fled at our attack would soon bring back the whole party, and we did not wish to encounter Cavalry in the Plains (Tyrrell 1916:262).

Thus, while still living as sedentary farmers in fortified earth-lodge villages on the eastern prairie fringe of the northern Plains, the Cheyennes had already, by 1780, incorporated the horse into their culture for both hunting and war. With a secure economy of maize, squash, and tobacco, balanced by large-scale communal hunting in which quantities of meat could be brought back on pack horses, the Cheyennes would have prospered mightily. And they could have stayed put, were it not for hostile neighbors and disease. When the able-bodied men and women went out onto the prairies to hunt on horseback, they could leave only a few braves behind to ride for help, if attacked. But as Sugar's story tells us, this was no adequate safeguard. Thus, the highly vulnerable sedentary villages were gradually abandoned, and some Cheyenne bands adopted the portable hide tipi as a mobile home which could be moved into close proximity to the herds as well as provide flexibility in seasonal adjustment to climatic conditions and the presence of enemies.

There was another important factor, too. The sedentary villages, with their crowded and ill-ventilated earth-lodges, each of which might house a dozen to thirty people in a single room, were deathtraps for a population which had no natural immunity to smallpox and measles, inadvertently brought in by the fur traders. Epidemics decimated the Mandan and Hidatsa villages in 1780 and 1782. These tribes responded not by giving up their ancient way of life, but by regrouping the survivors in a few new villages. The Cheyenne were more adaptable. Having already been detached from their traditional way of life a hundred years earlier, they simply took to their newly acquired horses and rode away from pestilence-ridden villages, which were incessantly harried by the Sioux and Chippewa, to seek survival in the open Plains.

THE PLAINS PHASE

Shortly after crossing the Missouri River in their westward movement, the Cheyennes encountered a strange tribe which had evidently been on the plains for some time. It was the Sutai. The Sutai, to the surprise of the Cheyennes, were found to speak a form of Algonkin which was so similar to Cheyenne that both tongues were mutually intelligible. After some initial hostilities, according to tradition, the two tribes became closely allied, until by 1820 the Sutai were looked upon merely as a distinctive band within the Cheyenne tribe.

Very early in the 1800s, the Black Hills in the northwest corner of South Dakota had become a spiritual Mecca to the wandering bands of Cheyennes. The rich verdure of the well-watered hills presented a striking contrast to the monotonous flats of the Dakota Plains. Bear Butte, an isolated hill, standing out on the plain northeast of the Black Hills, holds a cave which the Cheyennes incorporated into their beliefs as the place where the spirits taught the Cheyenne culture hero, Sweet Medicine, the tribal social and ceremonial organization, described in Part II of this book.

The various Cheyenne bands, however, moved about over a large area which formed a rough semi-circle to the west, south, and east of the Black Hills.

In the west, the Cheyennes fought regularly with the Crows and Wind River Shoshones, whose hunting grounds the Cheyennes were penetrating. Those bands which drifted southward through eastern Wyoming and western Nebraska into eastern Colorado found themselves locked in combat with the Ute, Comanche, and Kiowa tribes. Behind the Cheyennes, ever more aggressive and predatory Sioux kept up their expansionistic drive, until they had themselves finally (by 1850) engulfed all of South Dakota, including the Black Hills, and large parts of North Dakota, Nebraska, and eastern Wyoming.

The second third of the nineteenth century brought about a period of stabilization of Cheyenne movements and military arrangements. On the west, the great wall of the Rocky Mountains raised a barrier beyond which lay the Great Basin Desert—an uninviting territory, to say the least. In the south, between 1828 and 1832, William and George Bent, in company with Ceran St. Vrain, established an important trading post on the Arkansas River in southeastern Colorado, at a point suggested by the Cheyenne chief, Yellow Robe. The southern bands of Cheyennes moved from the Platte River down to the Arkansas in order to establish a stronger position as the tribe which would have primary access to the Bents' American artifacts. In 1840, the Cheyennes made a permanent peace with the Kiowas and Comanches in order to consolidate their southern position against the Pawnee and the newly-arrived tribes from the East, such as the Cherokee. They also wanted to obtain horses from their new allies, which they could themselves trade with the Bents for American goods.

In the north, the Cheyennes arranged a peace and alliance with the Sioux, who were willing now to join them in pressing the Crows and Shoshones against the mountains.

From this time on, the solidarity of the Cheyennes was stretched thin by the great distances separating the northernmost from the southernmost bands. It became more and more difficult for the tribe to assemble as a unit for the early summer Great Ceremonies. And this meant that the Tribal Council could convene less frequently and exercise only decreasing power over the entire tribal population.

One of the last of the great ceremonial gatherings of the entire Cheyenne nation was held in late August, 1842, on the banks of the South Fork of the Platte River, near Fort Lancaster in southeastern Wyoming, midway between the northern and southern bands.

During the period we have described thus far, the Cheyennes were never in direct conflict with the Whites. Settlers had not yet begun to penetrate the western plains, and traders were eagerly welcomed.

The United States victory over Mexico in the War of 1846 resulted in the loss of New Mexico, Arizona, and California to the United States. Santa Fe became an important center for North Americans, to be reached by overland trail from Independence, Missouri. The trail ran directly through the southern hunting territories of the Cheyenne. At the same time, the discovery of gold in California opened the stampede of '49-ers along the Platte River trail farther north, through the very center of Cheyenne country.

In 1851, the United States undertook to stabilize the boundaries of the Sioux, Arapaho, Cheyenne, and other tribes, in an effort to stop the intertribal territorial wars, which had been initiated by the fur trade two hundred years earlier. An effort was also made to pay the tribes in cash and goods for the loss of lands and disruption of hunting and buffalo grazing caused by emigrant trains and troop movements. The result was the Fort Laramie Treaty, through which the southern Cheyenne bands were, for purposes of the United States Government, joined in a single landholding unit with the Arapaho tribe, separate and distinct from the northern Cheyenne bands.

Henceforth, the Northern Cheyenne and Southern Cheyenne would, in terms of their political and legal arrangements with each other and the United States, exist as two distinct entities. Their historical experiences from then to the present day would move on divergent paths.

PART TWO

Climax
(1800–1850)

A. Ritual and Tribal Integration

To give the feel of the Cheyennes at the climax of their lifeway, this section is written in the ethnographic present. It is as though we have been carried back a hundred and fifty years through a time machine. But the result is not fiction. It is as accurately descriptive as scientific ethnography can make it.

2 / The great ceremonies

THE ARROW RENEWAL

At the time of the Renewal of the Sacred Arrows the summer sun is at its highest; its rising is farthest north on the eastern horizon; its position at noon is as close to the zenith as it can come. Spring has run its course; it is roughly the time of the summer solstice. The life-giving forces have waxed to their fullest strength.

On a broad, yet sheltered, flat near a good stream of water, where there is plenty of forage for the horse herds, the entire Cheyenne tribe gathers to renew its vitality. Eight hundred to a thousand tipis are raised in a great open circle, in the form of the new moon. They form a broad crescent with the gap between the horns facing the northeast, the point of the rising sun. The entrance of each family tipi also faces east, so that the sun's first rays will shine into the lodge. In the clear, open space of the great camp circle stand three isolated tipis. In the center is a huge, conical skin lodge, the Sacred Arrow Lodge. Off to the right is the lodge of the Sacred Arrow Keeper. At the edge of the open space, behind the Sacred Arrow Lodge, is the Offering Lodge, which is the tipi of the pledger of the ceremony.

In the great circle of family tipis, the lodges are grouped by bands. Each of the ten major bands of the Cheyennes camps together as a unit within the whole. Throughout the long winter, the bands, and even the family groups within the bands, have been scattered in smaller camps hidden in cottonwood groves along the watercourses, many miles apart. When spring was once more upon the land, an enterprising Cheyenne had made the rounds of all the camps. Sometime during the previous year, he had assumed the responsibility of organizing the Medicine (or Sacred) Arrow Renewal Rite. He had made a pledge or vow to the supernatural forces to do this thing. His kinsmen had helped him accumulate the necessary food and gifts. He had taken his ceremonial pipe and sufficient tobacco. He had traveled across the plains, seeking out every Cheyenne encampment, convening with the camp chiefs, offering them his pipe, and telling them of the place where the Arrow Renewal would be held.

Through the first weeks of summer, the bands had been steadily moving in toward the rendezvous, as if drawn by strands of invisible thread radiating out from a single center. Each band had stopped four times on its journey to pray and, in solemn ceremony, to smoke to the four directions and to the Great Medicine Spirits above. On the day before arriving at the appointed place, they had halted to don their finest clothing. Scouts from the main camp, where the pledger's people had been getting everything in readiness, had reported their approach. Their horses groomed and painted, themselves in full paint and finery, they had approached the spot of the camp circle from the east, riding in a long column, singing songs of happiness. All those who had reached the camp ahead of them had turned out in force to cheer and applaud them as they paraded around the camp circle and then went to the section of the arc traditionally reserved for them. Their women had quickly unloaded the pack horses; soon their lodges had been raised, and the cooking fires started. Invitations to meals had been sent back and forth, and friends and relatives had had a busy round of visiting, gossiping, eating, and gambling.

Now, however, not a sound may be heard in the camp, save the murmur of voices of the priests in the Medicine Arrow Lodge, or of the ceremonial drumming and singing that comes through the skins of the lodge. No one is to be seen, except the members of a warrior society silently pacing the rounds of the camp. An occasional man may emerge from his tipi quietly to go out on a necessary task. Women and children remain silent behind the closed coverings of the lodges. Even the dogs make no sound. Should one so much as growl or yelp, his skull is shattered with a swift blow of a patrolling warrior's club. In the great lodge, the priests have opened the fox-skin bundle in which the four Sacred Arrows are kept. It is the moment of supreme sacredness of the Cheyenne as a people. It is the moment at which the well-being of the tribe as a whole is in the process of renewal. The ordinary individual is but a minute particle that must suspend its activities in the solemnity of an activity that focuses on the life of the society.

The Medicine Arrows (*Mahuts*) symbolize the collective existence of the tribe. In a sense, they may be called the embodiment of the tribal soul. As the Arrows prosper, the tribe prospers; as they are allowed to suffer neglect, the tribe declines in prosperity. Their attributes are not in their material form, but in their ineffable supernatural qualities. Or in another sense, they may properly be called the supreme tribal fetish, a set of objects in which resides a spiritual power that belongs to all the people and is revered by all. The Arrows were given to the Cheyennes by their mythological culture hero, Sweet Medicine (*Mutsoyef*), who is believed to have brought to the Cheyennes many of their ways. He had been a strange and handsome youth with mysterious habits. As a married man, in his early maturity, he had journeyed with his wife to the Sacred Mountain[1] by the Black Hills. There, in a great cave, he had sat with the selected wise men of all the peoples of the earth as a pupil to Maiyun (the personified great spirit). Maiyun gave four arrows to Sweet Medicine and instructed him in their care and use. Two of these arrows have power over buffalo and two have power over human beings. When the buffalo Arrows are ritually pointed toward animals, they become confused and helpless, are easily surrounded and killed. When the Arrows are carried against an enemy tribe on the rare occasions when the Cheyenne go on the warpath with all the tribe along,[2] the man Arrows are ritually pointed at the enemy before the attack. The foe becomes blinded and befuddled. Thus, the Arrows are the

[1] Bear Butte, now a South Dakota State Park, located near Sturgis, S.D.

[2] The Medicine Arrows have been carried on tribal movements against enemies six times. The first was against the Shoshones in 1817; then against the Crows in 1820, the Pawnees in 1830, the Kiowas in 1838, the Shoshones in 1844, and finally, once again against the Pawnees in 1853.

Cheyennes' greatest resource against their most besetting manifest anxieties: failure of the food supply and extermination by enemies. The Arrows, as the supernaturals' great gift to the Cheyennes, are their central insurance for survival. For all their consummate skill as hunters and warriors, they know full well they cannot succeed all the time. In spite of their best efforts, starvation haunts them. In spite of their wily skill at arms, their braves are turned back defeated, their camps surprised, their horses run off, their people slain, scalped, or led off into captivity. The Arrows are proof against ultimate disaster, an assurance that in spite of everything all *will* prosper.

The Sacred Arrow Renewal is not an annual ceremony. In off years, either the Sun Dance or the Animal Dance (Massaum) will be performed in its stead. The Arrow Renewal Rite is pledged by an individual who wishes to do a great thing. It is a commitment to the supernaturals, undertaken as a vow under great stress or anxiety. A man who hopes for the recovery of a close kinsman, a brother, son, or wife, may promise to sponsor a Renewal. A man who is himself deathly sick may vow to do it if he survives. A warrior in mortal danger may be the one to vow to undertake it. These are voluntary acts, but done always under the duress of threatened personal loss. Under one circumstance, upon which we will elaborate later on, it is absolutely imperative that a Renewal be pledged and performed as soon as possible. This is when one Cheyenne has killed another. Murder within the tribe is the most horrendous of crimes and sins. Not only does the murderer become internally polluted and begin to rot inside, but flecks of blood soil the feathers of the Arrows. Bad luck dogs the tribe, and all game shun its territory until atonement is made in the Renewal and clean feathers replace those that are sullied on the Arrows. These are the ostensible reasons for holding the ceremony, which lasts four days.

The first day is given over to the making of offerings and preparing the sacred Arrow Lodge. The Offering Lodge belongs to the pledger and is raised by his wife. People bring what they wish to give to Maiyun. These items (usually robes, colored cloth, utensils, and food) are hung together on a pole in front of the lodge, or over its door. Early in the afternoon, all the warriors gather to select the spot for the Sacred Arrow Lodge. This done, they choose from among their number enough men of unspotted reputations to go out and cut a supply of extra-large lodge poles. The next job is to get a covering. The warriors appoint a delegation to visit two men who have been brave in war, generous, good, and even-tempered throughout their lives. These exemplars of Cheyenne virtue are singled out and honored with a request for the loan of the covers of their tipis to use on the Sacred Arrow or Renewal Lodge. When the huge lodge (which is about twice the size of a normal tipi) has been raised and covered, the Arrow Keeper and his associated priests enter it, strip off the sod, and smooth out the ground. They prepare a hearth in the center and a ceremonial sand altar (a mound) near the rear of the tipi. Sage, which is always a ceremonial purifier, is laid around the outer edges of the space; upon it the medicine men will sit.

On the second morning, the priests take their places in the Sacred Arrow Lodge. The pledger of the ceremony, naked except for a buffalo robe, his body painted red, leads three other good men to the Offering Lodge. The sacrificial gifts are removed from their position and carried single file into the Sacred Arrow Lodge, where they are placed as an offering before the altar. The four men then leave the lodge, walking slowly in the direction of the Sacred Arrow Keeper's tipi, wailing and keening as they go. Before the tipi door they advance and retreat four times before entering. The Arrow Keeper awaits them. They sit. He prays for them. The Arrow Bundle is then placed in their custody. In single file before the Keeper's tipi, they pray again as the pledger holds the bundle on his left arm. Slowly, very slowly, they move off in the direction of the Renewal Lodge. The mystic number four is observed again, as they halt four times on their traverse. In the lodge, the bundle is placed by the head priest on a prepared bed behind the altar. The ceremony proper is ready to begin; the warrior patrols begin their rounds of the camp, and we are now at the point at which we came upon the camp in the opening of this description.

Within the Renewal Lodge the secret rituals preparatory to the opening of the bundle are begun. At last, with great care, the bundle is unwrapped and the Arrows exposed and examined. If the feathers are not in perfect condition, a man who has lived in accordance with Cheyenne ideals is appointed to undertake the great task. He must be healthy, clean, good tempered, kind, generous, wise, and brave, never guilty of a dishonorable act. The work of renewal is performed on the third day.

The main performance of the third day symbolizes the unity of all the individual Cheyenne families in the one great entity—the tribe. A willow tally stick a yard long is prepared for every living Cheyenne family, save those who have produced a murderer. The counting sticks are laid in a pile beside the altar. In front, and to the side of the main fireplace, are two small incense fires that are kept aglow throughout the entire ceremony. One by one, the family counting sticks are smoked in the incense to bless every family individually and to give it well-being. During this part of the ceremony, all the medicine men in the camp are going through their private rituals of renewing the supernatural power of their medicine paraphernalia.

On the fourth and final day, the Arrows are exposed to the sun, and to public view. The pledger of the ceremony obtains a forked pole which he ritually carries into the Arrow Lodge. There the high priest affixes the Arrows to the pole. Wailing as he slowly walks from the lodge to a point some distance in front of the door, the pledger carries the pole and Arrows into the open. After he has returned to the lodge for the skin wrapper, which is placed on the ground before the pole, the priests bring forth the offerings that have been resting in the lodge. Boys bring additional offerings from their homes to place alongside the pole, as well. Now, while all the women are securely hidden in their tipis, every Cheyenne male, from the smallest babe in arms to the oldest dodderer, passes before the Arrows to receive their beneficent effect. They may look at the Arrows, but they are hard to see, for they give off a shining, blinding light. When all the males have passed before the Arrows, the warriors dismantle the Sacred Arrow Lodge, which is then set up over the Arrows and the offerings where they stand. This time, however, a third tipi cover is added to the original two, so that a lodge large enough to crowd in all the medicine men of the tribe is formed. The new lodge is called Sweet Medicine's Lodge, the home of the culture hero himself. The Sacred Arrows are now removed from this lodge and returned to the tipi of the Sacred Arrow Keeper, who holds his sacred office for life. In the meantime, a sweat-bath lodge is erected on the spot where the Offering Tipi had stood.

On the fourth and final night, the head chief of all the Cheyennes, who is himself called the Sweet Medicine Chief and thus represents the culture hero, enters the Sweet Medicine Lodge, followed by all the medicine men. They solemnly sing the four sacred songs that Maiyun had taught Sweet Medicine in the sacred mountain. After each song, they prophesy the future of the Cheyennes, even as Sweet Medicine had done when he returned to the tribe after his stay in the mountain. At long last, just before daybreak, all the participants repair to the sweat lodge for a steam bath which ritually decontaminates them, so that they may resume ordinary living and go among the women and children without danger. When the bath is finished, it is the dawn of the fifth day. After four days of confinement, the women may throw back the door coverings of their tipis and emerge into the open. Life is renewed, purified, and strengthened because it has been resanctified. Now the great communal hunts may follow.

A great tribal undertaking such as this has a number of aspects and effects:

1. It emphasizes the dependence of human beings (the Cheyennes) upon the beneficent help of the supernatural world. It reinforces the assumption that all that is good and desirable comes from the mystic beings.

2. It restates the norms of right conduct in individual and group life as formulated by Sweet Medicine in the long ago. The prophecies tell how the Cheyennes will prosper, if they act in the right way, and what will befall them, if they do not. To the sacred authority of tribal custom it adds the sanctity of ancient origin. It also singles out for signal honor men who are neither chiefs nor priests but whose lives have conformed to the ideal.

3. It guarantees the authority of the tribal chiefs, especially of the head chief, who, by virtue of his possession of the Sweet Medicine Bundle given to the tribe by Sweet Medicine himself, is the living incarnation of the long-dead creator of the Cheyenne way, Sweet Medicine.

4. It reinforces the authority of the old men of the tribe in general and all medicine men in particular.

5. It stamps the domination of males over females in ultimate determination of tribal matters, since men alone may actively participate in the rite.

6. Finally, and above all, it functions as the great symbolic integrator of the tribe, ritually demonstrating that the tribe, although its group components are the kindred (represented by the counting sticks), is more than the sum of its parts and that the parts must not act in a way that will sever the whole. (Separatist and disruptive tendencies in Cheyenne life will be discussed later.) In a more pragmatic and less symbolic manner, this concept is sustained in another way in the great communal buffalo hunt upon which the Cheyennes launch themselves as soon as the ritual is over.

THE SUN DANCE

The Sacred Arrows and the rite of their renewal are unique to the Cheyennes. Not so the Sun Dance, which is a ceremony common to most Plains Indian and a few Great Basin tribes. The central features of the Sun Dance are the same among all tribes, but there are many differences in the details of the ritual. Above all, the meaning and some of the secondary functions of the ceremony differ from tribe to tribe (see Bennett 1944).

The central theme of the Cheyenne Sun Dance is world renewal. As explained to G. A. Dorsey by a Cheyenne priest,

The object of the ceremony is to make the whole world over again, and from the time the Lodge-maker makes his vow everything is supposed to begin to take on new life, for the Medicine-Spirit [Maiyun], having heard the prayer of the pledger, begins at once to answer it. When the man makes the vow, he does it not so much for himself or his family, as for the whole tribe. Attending upon his vow and its fulfillment is an abundance of good water and good breath of the wind, which is the same as the breath of the Medicine-Spirit who regards all things. At the time of the Lone-tipi, when the earth is first created, it is just beginning to grow. As the ceremony progresses, this earth increases in size, and when the lodge itself is erected we build a fire which represents the heat of the sun, and we place the lodge to face the east that the heavenly bodies may pass over it and fertilize it (Dorsey 1905:II, 186).

The Cheyennes' own name for the Sun Dance embodies this notion in the word *oxheheom,* which means "New Life Lodge," or "Lodge of the Generator." Again, in the words of a Cheyenne priest,

Formerly this dance represented only the creation of the earth. The Cheyenne grew careless and combined other things with the ceremony. At the time of the Lone-tipi, though everything is barren, the earth is beginning to grow. Now it has grown. Thus they make the earth, buffalo wallow, grease, wool, and sinew to make growth. By the time of the end of the lodge things have grown, people have become happy; the world has reached its full growth, and people rejoice. When they use the bone whistle they are happy like the eagle, which is typical of all birds and of all happiness (Dorsey 1905:II, 57).

The origin myth of the Sun Dance attributes its introduction among the Cheyennes to a second culture hero, Erect Horns (*Tomsivsi*). He, like Sweet Medicine, journeyed to a sacred mountain near a great body of water to receive instruction from Maiyun and the Thunder Spirit. Unlike Sweet Medicine, however, he undertook his pilgrimage because of the dire need of the people. The myth tells that long ago there was famine. "Vegetation withered, the animals starved, the land became barren and dry, and the ancient Cheyenne were on the verge of starvation, for they had no food but dried vegetation and their dogs of burden" (Dorsey 1905:I, 46). Erect Horns was a young man then known as Standing on the Ground and also as Rustling Corn. He selected the beautiful wife of the tribal chief to slip off secretly with him on a long journey which led to the Sacred Mountain. Inside the mountain the pair was taught the Sun Dance. At the end, the Great Spirit gave Erect Horns the sacred horned buffalo-skin hat whence comes his name.

The spirit's parting words were,

Follow my instructions accurately, and then, when you go forth from this mountain, all of the heavenly bodies will move. The Roaring Thunder will awaken them, the sun, moon, stars, and the rain will bring forth fruits of all kinds, all the animals will come forth behind you from this mountain, and they will follow you home. Take this horned cap to wear when you perform the ceremony that I have given you, and you will control the buffalo and all other animals. Put the cap on as you go from here and the earth will bless you (Dorsey 1905:I, 48).

It was as it had been promised. When they came forth from the mountain, the entire earth turned fresh and new. The buffalo came forth to follow them to their homeland. The first Sun Dance was performed in accordance with Erect Horns' instructions, and all was well. The Buffalo Hat, which had been given to Erect Horns, is preserved to this day, and it constitutes the second great tribal fetish.

The Sun Dance was in fact introduced into Cheyenne culture by the Sutai, who still retain distinctive customs in dress and other matters. The Sun Dance prayers and songs are performed in the Sutai dialect rather than in true Cheyenne. Thus, the separate culture heroes, sacred tribal fetishes, and their associated ceremonies have been integrated into the tribal culture as two homologous complexes.

The Sun Dance of the Cheyenne has been recorded in considerable detail by Dorsey (1905:II) and Grinnell (1923). For our purposes no more than a brief indication of its major aspects need be recounted.

The ceremony is pledged by an individual for the same personal reasons as lead a person to sponsor the Sacred Arrow Renewal. The dance is usually given in years when there is no Arrow Renewal, but if both are to be given in the same season, the Sun Dance follows the Arrow Renewal, which is the more important ceremony.

The Sun Dance requires eight days to complete. The first four days are given over to building the dance lodge and to secret rites in the Lone Tipi, which symbolizes the Sacred Mountain. The last four days are devoted to the public dance in the Sun Dance Lodge.

The pledger is called "The Reproducer" or "Multiplier," because through his act the tribe is reborn and increases in numbers. From the time of making the vow until the completion of the dance, the pledger and his wife must not express their sexual desires. Any intercourse on their part will cause them to die. In the origin myth, Erect Horns refused to have sexual relations with his beautiful companion until after they had emerged from the Sacred Mountain. In preparing the ceremony, the pledger is helped not so much by his relatives as by the members of his warrior society, who give many gifts to defray the expense, and who themselves participate in the dance. They also direct certain phases of the ceremony. First, they direct the positions of the different bands in the camp circle. More important, they select from among the former Sun Dance priests the one who will enact the role of the Great Spirit, who first taught the ceremony to Erect Horns. He is known as "The One Who Shows How," and he serves as the high priest of the rite. He is helped by an assistant high priest, who represents Thunder, the second teacher of Erect Horns. The other priests are those men who have previously pledged the rite and so have learned the mysteries of the Lone Tipi. All of these men together, including the pledger, are called "The Reanimators."

The four days in the Lone Tipi are replete with symbolic imagery and actions portraying earth renewal and continuance. Five separate "earths" are successively smoothed out on the ground. A buffalo skull is ritually consecrated through the insertion of balls of water grass in its eye sockets and nostrils. Many special pipe cleaners—sticks with a wad of buffalo hair—represent the life-sustaining buffalo and must be changed after the rituals at each "earth," because they would carry away some of the power of growth of the earth if moved from one to another. The wife of the pledger (or some other woman chosen by him, if for any reason, such as menstruation, his own wife may not serve) shares the rites in the Lone Tipi with the high priest, just as Erect Horns' female companion was in the Sacred Mountain with him. The Lone

Tipi rites, like the Arrow Renewal Ceremony, end with a ritual, purificatory sweat bath for the priests.

The basic features of the public dance divide into four distinguishable parts: 1) the building of the lodge, 2) the priests' rituals, 3) dancing before the center pole, and 4) individual self-torture as a kind of sacrificial offering.

During the four preliminary days of the Lone Tipi rites, the remainder of the camp is not idle. The military society of the pledger, which is to dance as a body, sets up a tipi of one of its members in the open area within the circle. The pledger's society and others rehearse Sun Dance songs; they feast and exchange presents. Various families exchange feasts and gifts. Purely social dances are held for the fun of it. There is much socializing, gaming, expression of fun, and happiness. Such an atmosphere pervades the whole camp throughout the entire ceremony, except for the moments when the high priest and pledger's wife sexually consecrate themselves.

For the building of the lodge, a spy is first selected to find a suitable tree for the center pole. It must be some warrior who has penetrated into an enemy camp to scout them out on some occasion when the entire Cheyenne tribe was on the warpath. He selects the spot at which the center pole will be erected (somewhere out toward the front of the open area within the camp circle). Here he puts up a few willow boughs. Next he goes out on the "warpath" to find an "enemy." Stealthily penetrating a grove of trees, he spots a suitable tree, steals up on it and counts coup with his ax upon its trunk. (Coup is the French word meaning "blow." A coup is any honorable war deed at the expense of a Cheyenne enemy.) All this is done on the second and third days.

On the morning of the third day, the scout circles the camp before approaching the center pole markers. These he strikes and tells of the war exploit that qualified him for his select honor. Meanwhile, the braves of the different military societies are dressing and putting on their war paint. One after another, each society rides full tilt into the camp circle, whooping and shouting. Armed with willow spears and shields, they charge straight at the center pole boughs, striking them as they charge past, subsequently to engage in sham battles. Women, too, gather to count coup on the enemy. Then all go off to cut the timbers for the lodge. Each of four military societies brings in a specially painted pole to represent the four directions. It is a time of great excitement and high spirits.

The center pole is cut and transported ritually by chiefs only, for it represents the world and "the sunshine of all the world." It is the last of the upright poles to be put in place, and its raising is done with much ritual and sacrificial offerings. Bundles of dogwood and cottonwood brush are lashed between the two forks of what is to be the upper end of the center pole. They become the nest of the Thunder-bird, the spirit who controls the sun and rain, and is the chief of all birds. A broken arrow, symbolic of enemy arrows which are thus made useless, a bit of buffalo meat, symbolic of the major food supply, a rope representation of the morning star, and a phallic rawhide effigy of an enemy tribesman are added to the nest. In raising the pole, songs are sung which relate to the growth of the earth.

The completed lodge forms a large circle of upright posts around the center pole to which they are joined by stringers. The roof is partially covered over with valuable buffalo robes donated by qualified warriors. On the night of the day it is finished, the lodge is dedicated by the priests, who sing eight groups of ceremonial songs for the dancers who perform set and restrained rhythmic patterns. Now the great act of regenerative consecration is offered. The chief priest and wife of the pledger step together over incense, enveloping themselves in a buffalo robe so that they will be thoroughly purified throughout their bodies by the sacred incense. This done, the priests all file from the lodge, led by the pledger's wife. To the east of the lodge and just inside the opening of the camp circle they stop. A solemn prayer is offered to Maiyun, to the spirits of the four directions, to the sun and stars. It asks their blessing on the entire world. It begs for the growth of the world, for animals, birds, and people, for blessing upon stones, trees, grass, and earth of all kinds, and that the sun shall shine and rain shall fall, as needed.

The priests return to the Sun Dance Lodge, leaving the high priest and pledger's wife alone. Now the Crier, who is one of the priests purified and painted, calls upon all the world to listen as he announces the right of the high priest to perform the ritual act he is about to do on behalf of the tribe. The priest and pledger's wife draw the buffalo robe about themselves, incensing their bodies again. They sing the sacred pipe song and "grow" the earth, raising the sacred pipe skyward four times. Within the robe they then have sex relations, so that all that lives may be born. Now the dance proper may begin.

In the dancing, the participants face the center pole, rising up and down on their toes while standing in one place. As they rise, they blow piping, short blasts upon eagle-wing bone whistles held between their teeth. Those who can endure it to the end do so almost continuously (with but brief periods of rest and without food or water) for four nights and days. On each day, they are ceremonially painted with a series of symbolic painted patterns applied by ceremonial grandfathers.

On the following day, the priests, assisted by the wives of the pledger and high priest, go through an elaborate ritual of building an altar within the dance lodge. It is built around the sacred buffalo skull that had been prepared in the Lone Tipi, and includes five pieces of sod (growing grass) symbolic of the five great directional spirits, arched sticks (rainbows), brush (the matured vegetation for which they have prayed in the Lone Tipi), and a sandpainting symbol of the morning star in red, black, yellow, and white sand. Peeled sticks, painted white and representing scalped enemies, are there, too, as are feathered, red and black painted sticks representing the Cheyennes.

The altar symbolizes the fifth earth made in the priests' rituals; it is the completed and realized earth toward which the whole ceremony is directed— an earth replete with green life and buffalo, sunshine and rainbows, beneficent spirits, healthy Cheyennes and defeated enemies. It is the supreme hope.

To the untutored outsider who sees the public aspects of the Cheyenne Sun Dance, the most spectacular part (and in the view of a number of early reporters, a horrifying thing) is the voluntary self-torture undertaken by a number of the men. Self-torture is practiced by a number of northern Plains tribes as a form of religious sacrifice, but none carry it to the degree practiced by the Cheyennes. A few of the dancers in the Sun Dance Lodge may indulge in it, but most of the sufferers perform their acts of self-sacrifice outside of the lodge. The sacrifice is made as the result of a voluntary, individual vow in the hopes of obtaining the "pity" of supernatural spirits, and thus achieving good fortune. The act also brings great public approval and is a conspicuous means of gaining social prestige.

The self-sacrifice in the dance lodge is known as "hanging from the center pole." One who has vowed to do this asks a medicine man who has himself made the same sacrifice to help him. The medicine man fastens the end of two ropes to the crotch of the center pole, adjusting them so that they will reach just to the breast height of a standing man. He next punches or cuts two holes in the skin just above each nipple. A small skewer is pushed through each pair of holes so that a narrow strip of skin laps over it and holds it against the breast. The free ends of the rope are fastened about the skewers. The sacrificer may then dance, fastened to the pole, all through the night, and if by morning he has not succeeded in tearing the skin loose so as to free himself, his medicine man cuts the skin off, and his ordeal is ended. Or, if the sacrificer wishes to achieve his end in one sudden burst, he may suddenly strain back on the ropes in an effort to tear the skewers free at once. There are variations and elaborations on this pattern: skewers may be put through the flesh of the face over the cheekbones just below the eyes; skewers from which are hung buffalo skulls may be put into the shoulders and over the shoulder blades on the back. Those who do not wish to sacrifice themselves in the lodge will have skewers put in their backs. Ropes are hung from the skewers, and as many as from one to fifteen buffalo skulls are attached to the ropes. The sacrificer drags these along the ground around the camp circle. If the catching of the horns of the skulls in brush and grass does not cause the thongs to tear loose, the flesh is cut to release them when the sacrificer has trudged as long or as far as he has vowed.

Such self-sacrifice does not contribute to the earth-renewal purposes of the Sun Dance, nor is it done on behalf of the tribe as a whole. It may be vowed to help cure a relative or to avert danger in war. Or it may be undertaken as the result of a dream. The psychological basis of these practices will be discussed in Chapter 11.

THE MASSAUM (CONTRARY) OR ANIMAL DANCE

The third of the great tribal ceremonies is very different in quality from the Arrow Renewal and Sun Dance, although it, too, is intended to insure well-being—that is, plenty of meat. It is mainly a hunting ritual taught to Sweet Medicine when he visited the Sacred Mountain. He, in turn, brought it to the Cheyennes.[3] Women play a much more important role throughout the Massaum.

Four days and nights are given over to closed rites in a double-sized skin

---

[3] It is highly probable that the Cheyennes borrowed the idea of animal dancers, as well as self-torture in the Sun Dance, from the Mandan Indian Okeepa ceremony, which they would have had occasion to see during the period of their stay on the Missouri River. For a first-hand description of the Okeepa, see Catlin 1967.

tipi raised about a center pole on which green boughs have been left, "that all the trees and grass and fruits may grow strong." The pledger and his wife are under the instruction of a priest who has previously pledged the dance. There are the many ritual movements of smoking, painting, and so forth (described in detail in Grinnell 1923:II, 285–334). In this case, all activity centers on preparing and painting a wolf skin to be worn by the pledger on the fifth and final day.

In private lodges, various men who have dreamed of some animal acting in a peculiar way get a group of their friends ritually to dress up in imitation of this animal. On the fourth day, women build a symbolic antelope or buffalo corral—a shaded pen of upright poles with two diverging arms of brush extending out toward the opening of the camp circle.

Two wolves are the main ritual animals, but on the fifth day other groups join in—buffalo, elk, deer, foxes, mountain lions, horses, bears, antelope, coyotes, and cranes and blackbirds. The men of each group run, dance, and act like the animal they represent. The animals run about, "hunted" by members of the Bowstring Society, or Contrary Warriors, who do things backwards and are the bravest of the brave. In the Animal Dance, they clown and cut up to the delight of the people watching. Hence, the dance is called Massaum, derived from *massa'ne,* crazy. At various points, the animals enter the corral, which is just what the Cheyenne want the animals to do when they use this method of hunting (see pp. 69–70). All this mimicry and clowning, which occurs on the final day, involves a great amount of high jinks and sporting fun, and is thus a great contrast to the heavy solemnity of the Arrow Renewal and the strenuous self-sacrifice of the Sun Dance. The four days and nights of preliminary rites, however, are not unlike those preceding the Sun Dance in general character and in details (including, *apparently,* the sexual dedication of the pledger's wife with the instructing high priest).

Whichever dance, or dances, may be given in any particular year, when the ceremony is over the whole tribe is ready to move off on the great summer buffalo hunt. Their spirits are high and they are ready to act as one body, confident now in their powers, for the whole earth and all upon it has been reinvigorated in their favor, and their mastery over their environment and all the animals in it is complete.

THE SACRED HAT

Second only to the Medicine Arrows as a sacred tribal symbol of great power is the Medicine Hat, made of buffalo fur from the top of a buffalo's head with the horns attached. The hat itself is not known to be the center of any great tribal religious ceremony, but it is endowed with a number of special powers and is held in great reverence. It is believed to have been in the possession of the Sutai tribe before it became consolidated within the Cheyenne, and its keeper must be of Sutai descent. The hat is kept in a large bundle in its Keeper's tipi, and is carried on the back of his wife whenever the tribe moves.

The Hat Keeper's lodge is a place of asylum where any enemy is safe (if he can reach it!), and the Hat has other protective features associated with it.

One of these is a piece of hair-fringed leather, called *Nimhoyeh*, or The Deflector. When carried in battle, it turns away arrows, spears, and bullets. Ritually used, it also wards off diseases. On rare occasions, when the entire tribe moves out on the war path, the Medicine Hat is carried into battle.

B. Social Structure

3 / Family, kindred, and band

By social structure is meant the ways in which groups and individuals are organized and relate to each other in the functioning entity that is the society. Among the Cheyennes the most significant groups are the family, kindred, band, women's societies, military fraternities, and the tribal council of forty-four peace chiefs.

COURTSHIP AND MARRIAGE

Marriage, for the Cheyennes, is a formal and serious matter. The Cheyennes are sexually repressed, have very strict notions of proper conduct, and are most sensitive to what other members of the tribe think of them. In the story of her life, a Cheyenne woman told Truman Michelson:

> My mother would always tell me that the main purpose of her teaching me, as well as the object of my owning my own bed, was to keep me at home, and to keep me from being away to spend my nights with my girl chum. This was done so that there would be no chance for gossip by other people (Michelson 1932:2).

When, as a girl, this woman first began to get the attentions of a beau, her father's sister came to her lodge to instruct her in how a girl should act and to stress the importance of proper behavior. Even when marriage was finally achieved, the situation did not change very much. "After I was married I thought I would have more freedom in going around with my girl friends, but my mother watched me more closely and kept me near my husband, day and night. This was done to prevent any gossip from my husband's people" (Michelson 1932:7).

Her statement was not idle talk, nor was hers an unusual instance, for Grinnell is not overstating the case when he writes,

> The women of the Cheyennes are famous among all western tribes for their chastity. In old times it was most unusual for a girl to be seduced, and she who had yielded was disgraced forever. The matter at once became known, and she was taunted with it wherever she went. It was never forgotten. No young man would marry her (Grinnell 1923:I, 156).

Under such circumstances Cheyenne courting is a bashful and long, drawn-out affair. It usually takes four or five years for a young man to win his bride, and when he is ready to put the question it is directed to her family and not to the girl. What is more, good form requires that the young man not do the

27

asking himself but rather send an old female or other relatives in his stead. After adolescence, boys and girls do not associate with each other, so there is no direct opportunity to develop camaraderie. Once a boy has seen a girl whom he hopes to make his sweetheart, he approaches her furtively. He knows the path from her family lodge to the stream where she gets water or the grove where she gathers wood. Hopefully, he stands along the path. As she passes, he gives her robe a little tug. Perhaps he feels this is too bold. If so, he whistles or calls to her. She may stonily ignore him, much to his mortification. Or she may make the stars shine by stopping to talk about this and that, but never of love. If all goes well, they may later begin to meet and talk outside her lodge. In time, they may exchange rings (either the old-time horn ones or those of metal obtained from traders) that young people wear. They are then engaged. Except for the exchange of rings, a suitor rarely gives presents directly to a girl. When the time comes, these go to her male relatives.

Tootling on a medicine flute is supposed to be a means of casting a love spell over a reluctant maiden. Certain medicine men can concoct a spruce gum to help a hapless swain to win his goal. If the girl chews the gum, her thoughts cannot leave the boy who gives it to her.

In the course of time, a suitor makes his intention known to his close kindred. If they do not agree that the match is a good one, they will refuse to assist him. If they approve, they bring together such items as clothing, blankets, guns, bows and arrows, and horses. One or more elderly respected men or women are selected to lead the horses piled with gifts over to the tipi of the girl's parents. The horses are staked outside. The emissary enters, smokes, talks small talk, finally puts the question, and then goes home without waiting for the answer. This is because the girl's family has to have time to talk the matter over. Her father or brother, as the case may be, sends for her male kindred, who convene at her tipi to discuss the pros and cons of the match. Should they decide against it, the horses are led back to the suitor. Should they decide "Yes," the goods are unloaded and distributed among the relatives. On the next day, they all convene again, bringing gifts equivalent in worth to what each has received. While the women of the family paint and outfit the girl in her finest buckskin dress, the men load their gifts on the horses that are to be returned in exchange for those already received. The finest horse of all is reserved as the bride's mount. Thus richly caparisoned, she is led to the lodge of her husband-to-be by an old woman not a relative. Her mother follows, leading the gift horses. At the groom's lodge, his young relatives and friends place the bride on a blanket, carry her through the door, and bestow her in the place of honor at the rear of the tipi. There her new female in-laws re-dress her in the new clothes they have made for the occasion, redo her hair, and repaint her. A feast follows.

In the days following, both mothers work at providing a new household. It is the girl's mother's privilege to provide a new tipi and its furnishing. Relatives from both sides help with many contributions. When all is ready, the lodge is set up, usually in the vicinity of the bride's mother's lodge (uxorilocal residence). The couple then leave the husband's tipi for their own. Thus is a new secondary conjugal family founded (the primary conjugal family being the one into which a person is born).

THE COMPOSITE FAMILY

We have just noticed that when a Cheyenne couple marries they move into their own lodge, which has been made by the bride's mother and is located close by the lodge of the bride's parents. In the normal course of events, the lodges of the mother's married sisters are also pitched nearby. A loose residential complex of related women and their primary conjugal families is thus formed, and this residential practice does give the localized family group a slight *uterine* (mother, female) bias. On the other hand, the "head" of most families is normally the oldest active husband in the group. And he is one who has married in from the outside. Thus, as a functioning settlement group the uxorilocal, composite family consists of the head, his wife or wives, their sisters and their husbands in their separate lodges, their married daughters and their husbands in their lodges, plus all the unmarried children of the lot of them, and perhaps a few stray relatives. Their own married sons have moved off to settle in with their wives' composite families. Thus, it falls upon the sons-in-law to be the main providers of meat for all the home group. The meat is cooked at the mother's tipi and carried by the daughters to their own lodges for eating.

There is much cooperation among the members of a composite family in the chores of daily living, but a good deal of privacy for each conjugal family as well.

Families differ in social prestige. As Grinnell writes, "Family rank . . . depended on the estimation in which the family was held by the best people. A good family was one that produced brave men and good sensible women, and that possessed more or less property. A brave and successful man has raised his family from low to very high rank; or a generation of inefficient men might cause a family to retrograde" (Grinnell 1923:I, 129). The Cheyennes with whom I worked gave the following characteristics of a good family: 1) it has plenty of good riding horses (forty or fifty of them); 2) the wife is a good housekeeper who keeps everything about the tipi neat and clean, is always good natured, and gets up every morning in the same mood; 3) it has plenty of parfleches stocked with dried meat, possible (ditty) bags, and long fringed saddle bags, good clothes and robes, all "up to date" and in good order; 4) it raises nice children, "those who act right, speak respectfully to elders, and so on."

A poor family is thought to be one in which: 1) the man is a poor rustler (that is, has no ability to take enemy horses); 2) has only three or four horses, probably saddle worn and footsore from overuse; 3) has only a little food, a small tipi, and only enough clothes and robes to keep them warm. "Some poor men were hard workers but had no luck. People sometimes blame the wife. He rustles well, but she is wasteful" (Hoebel, n.d.).

KINSHIP BEHAVIOR AND TERMINOLOGY

The kinship structure of the Cheyennes is basically bilateral; its emphasis is on horizontal classification along generation levels rather than vertically along lineage lines (Eggan 1955:71). The Cheyennes draw no distinction between siblings and cousins. Within the primary conjugal family an emphasis on seniority is reflected in a distinction between elder brother (*na'niha*) and younger (*na:sima*), and elder sister (*namhan*) and younger (*na:sima*). The younger brothers and sisters are not distinguished from each other in terminology. Relative age is more important than the sex of the person referred to (if that person is younger). Hence, *na:sima* means younger sibling of either sex. The age distinction does not apply in the case of cousins, however; all of them are called either "brother" or "sister."

A Cheyenne calls his father, father's brother, and all known male cousins of his father *nihu'*. But the mother's brother, who perforce belongs to a different kindred, is called *naxan*. Although for convenience we have translated *nihu'* as father, what it really means to a Cheyenne is "male member of my male progenitor's kindred and generation." Father and paternal uncles are considered together as kinsmen of the same order, while maternal uncles are terminologically identified as being in a different category.

Mother, mother's sister, and mother's female cousins are all called *na'go'*, while father's sisters and father's female cousins are distinguished as *nahan*.

On the generation level of grandparents a Cheyenne draws no distinction other than sex: grandfather and grandmother, just as in the Anglo-American kinship system. Two generations below him, a Cheyenne makes no distinctions whatsoever. All related children are called *nixa*, grandchild.

A Cheyenne calls his own children *na:'* (son) and *na'ts* (daughter). He also calls the children of his brothers and male cousins by the same terms. In other words, they are equated with his own offspring. All are child members of the same extended family. The children of his sisters and female cousins he calls "nephew" and "niece." They are set apart. When a Cheyenne woman is talking, she calls her sisters' and female cousins' children by the son and daughter terms, while *she* sets apart the children of her brothers and male cousins as nephew and niece. Consequently, when a male is speaking, *na:'* and *na'ts* mean more than "son" and "daughter"; they mean "offspring of my male relatives of my own generation." What we have for convenience called "nephew" and "niece" really mean "offspring of my female relatives of my own generation." They must be called by a different term from that used by a Cheyenne to identify his own children; if they were called the same as son and daughter, it would logically imply that a man was producing children by his sisters— and that is forbidden by the incest prohibitions.

If the reader has grasped the nature of the way a Cheyenne groups his relatives as revealed by relationship terms, he will see that five things stand out as distinctive in the kinship structure: 1) both parents' kindred are equally important to the individual. He does not socially or legally belong to one group and not the other. There is no unilineal descent group. All kin of his own generation, whether descended on the mother's side or the father's are "brother" and "sister." 2) On the parental level, mother's brother and father's sister are given special terms, since they cannot marry one's "mother" or "father" and because they belong to different kindred from the father and mother respectively. 3) "Sons" and "daughters" and "nephews" and "nieces" belong to the same kindred, but have to be distinguished because of the implications of the incest taboo. 4) All "grandchildren" are lumped together, since, from the speaker's point of view, they are all members of the same extended kindred. 5) Grandparents are also lumped for the same reason as grandchildren.

The Cheyennes, therefore, tend to draw as few distinctions as possible between relatives, except for distinctions between generations (although Petter estimates that the twenty-eight relationship terms *can* be modified in over 20,000 ways [Petter 1915:900]). This is consonant with the emphasis on seniority in social relations which is so important in the authority system of their culture. As was shown in the first chapter, they think of the tribe as one large family (the camp circle, for example, symbolizes the family tipi). They extend the concept of the family as widely as possible. Marriage is much more a family than an individual matter. Family relations tend to be collective rather than individual.

Within the kinship group, however, the different statuses call for special modes of customary behavior. Husbands and wives, although they are diffident in their attitudes toward each other in the early stages of their marriages, usually become most fond of each other. They form a close working team with a strong sense of family responsibility. Michelson's old woman informant related, "We had our first child after we had been married a year. It was at that time that I began really to love my husband. He always treated me with respect and kindness" (Michelson 1932: 8). And when her husband died, "His death made me very lonely, and it was the most terrible event in my life." Such was the ideal life between husbands and wives, although of course, it did not always work out thus. Some wives were shrewish. Some men were jealous or mean tempered. A story is told of one such man, Brave Wolf.

Brave Wolf was jealous of his wife's good looks. He would hear people remarking, "There is a woman who has two children and still holds her looks." These were children she had had by her former husband, High-backed Wolf, who had been killed by the Crows. Angered one day, Brave Wolf whipped his wife, Corn Woman, and when the camp moved, he left her behind. Brave Wolf's nephew, Sun Road, then a single man, came by and heard her weeping. He went to his lodge to get his horse to bring the woman along. He brought her into the main camp that evening. Brave Wolf heard that she was there and came over to take up where he had left off. He began whipping her in her face.

Digging Bear, his niece, watched for her chance. She struck his arm with a club and numbed it as he raised it to swing his whip. He cried out, "Wait until my arm stops hurting! I'll fix you." Digging Bear told Corn Woman to get into the lodge. Brave Wolf got over his hurt and followed her into the lodge to whip her some more.

His niece started cracking his shins with a club.

"It's funny," Brave Wolf said, "that you children are taking the part of a woman not any relation to you. I am your uncle."

"Well, if you hadn't thumped our mother, we would not have done so." (Brave Wolf was their father's cousin and was hence called "father"; his wife was therefore their classificatory "mother," even though not a genetic relative.) Brave Wolf then took Corn Woman home, but the next morning he was thumping her again, so she ran away to hide in a gulch, covering herself with grass. Brave Wolf went riding up and down looking for her, with no success. When she thought she was safe, she went out and hid in a patch of boulders. The camp moved on in time, and she was left alone there starving.

After some time, a big wolf came up and asked her what was the trouble (he could speak good Cheyenne).

"My husband has been beating me, and I ran away."

"Well," the wolf told her, "I'll get you back safely."

He brought her meat, and warned her when a bear came by, so that she got safely up in a tree and could stay there until the bear went away. An elk came and talked to her, too. He gave her elk power.

Meantime, Brave Wolf went into mourning for her. Everyone in the camp thought she had committed suicide. Brave Wolf also joined the Contraries (a small group of recklessly brave men, who do everything backwards). He got a Contrary lance made by High Forehead. Only single men may have such a lance, but when Corn Women left Brave Wolf, he was single again. He tried to get himself killed in battle, but Contrary lances are very lucky and this one carried him safely through battles. He could not get himself killed.

After a long time, the wolf led Corn Woman back to the Cheyenne camp. The wolf and the woman sat on a high hill overlooking the camp. "Over there is the camp," said the wolf. "A man will come out to look for you. You can't see him. Now I leave you. From now on, always put out some meat for me each morning." For the rest of her days, Corn Woman made the offering to the wolf who had saved her; he was her guardian spirit. When the wolf left her, she "came to." Later, she told people she thought she had almost turned into a wolf herself.

Now she started down the hill through a gulch, and she met a young man. He saw her in her disheveled condition. No clothes but a small piece of blanket for covering. No hair comb. Her hair in a mess. She was weak and emaciated from lack of proper food. The sight of him made her weaker. She staggered. The young man was so sorry for her that he wept in pity. She tried to, too. But no tears or voice would come.

"You stay right here," he said. "Your brother is hunting right over there. I'll bring him."

He found Crazy Head, her brother, and told him, "Your sister is right over here."

Crazy Head and the hunters rushed over and found her. They carried her back to the camp on a horse, so weak she could hardly stay on it.

Brave Wolf heard the news. He came in, his hair cut in mourning style. He ran up and started to hug his former wife. She bit his arm.

That made Crazy Head mad. He wanted to kill Brave Wolf, because he had made his sister remain away for so long. Then Corn Woman's mother came up and started to beat Brave Wolf. All the people began beating him. When they got back in camp, all the women beat him.

Brave Wolf was infatuated with Corn Woman. He wanted her back. He kept sending horses for her, but Crazy Head's people would throw sticks at them and drive them away. Corn Woman's mother would insult the women who brought them. When Brave Wolf came around, Corn Woman's sister would strike him on the forehead and taunt him, saying, "You look more like a mountain sheep than a man." He made no effort to protect himself, but would only drop his head and take the blows.

Brave Wolf was a great fighter, not then a chief, though he was later. He had a fine black war pony that everyone wanted, but he would not trade it or give it away.

On the warpath, he took to cooking for Sun Road, Corn Woman's brother. He did everything for him, just as though he were a servant.

One time, when Crazy Head was leading a war party, Brave Wolf brought Sun Road a nice roast. He was leading the famous bob-tailed black. "You know I have ridden this horse in war. You know this horse's qualities as well as I do," he told Sun Road. "Now I want you to have him to ride in war. What is more, I want you to have my Contrary lance, if you will take it." These were his greatest possessions.

When they were back from the war party, Sun Road spoke to his mother, "You know that when a man is leading a war party he is apt to go pretty hungry so that his men will have enough to eat. Brave Wolf has done all these pitiful things for me. I have known all the time what he wants. He wants my sister back. You had better put up an extra lodge. My sister will go back to him. You tell her to get ready."

When her mother told her what Sun Road had said, Corn Woman wept. "I never thought I would marry that man again, but if my brother says I must go, I must. My brother is a great fighter. If I say, 'No,' he'll probably get himself killed in the first fight (a protest suicide). Then I'll think how I caused it."

When they were together again, she told Brave Wolf, "Don't you ever try to beat me again. If you do, I'll fight you with whatever is at hand. I don't care if you kill me."

From that time on, he was her slave.

This case history, which was told by Calf Woman (who was in the camp at the time) and confirmed by High Forehead, illustrates a number of aspects of Cheyenne society. First, Cheyennes, like any other human beings, are not automatic slaves of custom; there are always those who deviate from the norms of right conduct. But the Cheyennes as a group have an unusually strong sense of proper form and they are not prone to let misconduct pass lightly. Second, the wrong-doing Cheyenne who repents, is contrite, and is willing to make amends, is rehabilitated with the cooperation of his fellows and restored to his former state. Third, Cheyenne women, although their status is inferior to men in many respects, are strong willed and aggressive; they are by no means downtrodden. Fourth, the Cheyenne male who finds the stress of life too much may find an institutionalized way open to glory and public esteem by becoming a Contrary, or more simply by getting himself killed in battle, dying the glorious death. Fifth, brothers have an absolute right of disposition of their sisters in marriage, a right that takes precedence even over the father's (Corn Woman said she was afraid she would be responsible for her brother's suicide by death in battle if she did not accede to his decision).

The brother-sister relationship is one of formal respect and restraint. Although they may play together as small children, beginning at puberty they must shed all manifestations of familiarity. There can be no physical contacts or joking between them. No obscenities may be uttered in each other's presence. Indeed, they may not even speak to each other. There is an indirect way around this tabu, however. A man who goes to his brother-in-law's tipi to borrow something, for instance, may find that the brother-in-law is not at home. He does not tell his sister what he wants, but he can tell her little baby of his request. After a while his sister, having overheard his wish, puts the article in a place where it can be seen. He picks it up and departs. He has obtained what he wants without violating the amenities of right conduct.

The incest tabu applies rigorously to brothers and sisters, and governs all their conduct. This is consonant both with Cheyenne distrust of sex and with the universal functional bases of the incest tabus. It also correlates with the power of disposal in marriage that a brother may exercise over his sister. So great is this authority, and so serious an affront to a young brave's ego is its flaunting, that if a sister disobeys his word, a brother may actually commit suicide (and there have been such cases). In such a case, the girl is disowned by her family. Pemmican Road's sister was driven from the tribe for disobeying her brother. Many years later, she returned to the Northern Cheyenne. When people came to tell her father, the famous chief, Iron Shirt, that his daughter had returned, he stonily replied, "I do not know how many years have passed since I disowned her for disobeying her brother. She is not my daughter. I do not want to see her." She tried again later, but he never took her in. "Pemmican Road died without father or mother" (Llewellyn and Hoebel 1941:174–175).

A woman divorces her husband simply by moving back to her parents' tipi. A man may divorce his wife by drumming her away at the so-called Omaha Dance. At one point in the dance, those men who have drummed a wife away dance as a group. A man who wants publicly to shame his wife may join them. At the end of the dance he strikes the drum, crying, "I throw her away." When a man is made a leader of the Omaha Dance, the greatest gesture he can make is to throw his sister away. "It is like giving away a fine horse, only more so." In contrast to a wife so divorced, the sister is supposed to be highly honored. When a brother strikes the drum, he throws the stick among the men, and the man whom it hits becomes the sister's husband.

Mothers continually admonish, exhort, and train their daughters. Fathers are friendly with their sons, but do little about their education until they are of age; boys are pretty much on their own and learn from each other until it is time to go on the warpath. It is a father's sister who has the freer relation to a child. She makes the infant's cradle and gives it gifts throughout life. She lightly teases the children in a way a mother never does. A niece may make jokes in return and may use any of the aunt's property without asking, if she needs it. Throughout life, a niece gives her aunt presents in exchange for her privileges. All in all, the relation of children, both male and female, to their father's sister is free of the formal restraints they are made to feel toward their mother. "I would prefer to have an aunt around any time rather than my mother," was the way High Forehead summed it up. Mother's sisters are "mothers" and treated accordingly.

A maternal uncle has much the same relation to his nieces and nephews as does the father's sister. Unlike the system in many American Indian tribes in which he, rather than the father, punishes an unruly boy (Pettit 1946: 18–24), a Cheyenne mother's brother, although he will talk to the boy, will never punish him. Mothers sometimes lose patience with their daughters and strike them. In two recorded cases in which this happened, the daughter hanged herself and the mother was banished for murder; after these events the Arrows were renewed (Llewellyn and Hoebel 1941:1961–162).

Cheyenne grandparents are the great indulgers of the children. Allowing for the differences in their ages, grandparents and grandchildren are real comrades and treat each other quite as equals. Grandfathers pass the tribal lore and myths to their descendants.

In-law relations are of a different order. Cheyennes like to accrue relatives and they welcome the enlargement of their kinship bonds through marriage. It is because this is so important to them that the families take such care in approving and selecting the mates for their youngsters. In any society there is always an undercurrent of psychological hostility between in-laws. In some, such as Dobu, the hostility is overt and institutionally manifest (Fortune 1932). In Cheyenne culture, however, the institutions of social structure are devised to minimize and control the hostility while at the same time building up the cooperative aspects of the relationship.

A Cheyenne male calls his sister's husband *nitov.* He also calls his wife's brother by the same term. The term, which is equivalent to our "brother-in-law" descriptively means "brother through marriage or affinity." Brothers-in-law are expected to be rough and ready pals. They give assistance to each other (as the suitor on the warpath), exchange presents from time to time, and work together. This is the cooperative side. Hostility, on the other hand, is vicariously released through rough joking and horseplay. Once when the camp crier was making the rounds calling the tribal chiefs to council, Bull Head cried out, "Don't call them chiefs! Call them fools. There are too many fools with the chiefs." This was not blasphemy, for his brother-in-law was a chief; when I was told this anecdote by Last Walker, the other Cheyennes in the tent roared with laughter. It was a good brother-in-law joke, an expression of privileged familiarity much appreciated.

A man's attitude toward his sister-in-law is much like that toward brothers-in-law. They joke and are more than free and easy in their overt relations. The relations are just the opposite to those that exist between brother and sister. The incest tabu that restrains siblings is not present in this relationship; every sister-in-law is a potential second wife to a Cheyenne man, since the tribe practices preferential levirate and sororate marriage. Because the ties between the two families have already been cemented by marriage, the circumspect behavior of a boy courting his first wife-to-be need not apply in sister-in-law relations.

Behavior toward a man's mother-in-law, however, is quite a different matter. She is absolutely tabued to him. Although he has to furnish her household with meat and perform other services, he may never, never speak to her. He should never be alone with her, and when he is in her presence, he should cover his head. Familiarity is out of the question and the opportunities for development of friction between them are reduced to a minimum.

For some Cheyennes, however, the situation can be otherwise. A man who has performed well in all things receives considerable social approbation when he selects one of the horses he has taken in war to give to his mother-in-law. The presentation, of course, is made through another person. His mother-in-law may then return the honor, if she is a member of the Robe Quillers Society. To do this she makes him a fine buffalo robe embroidered in dyed porcupine quills, which she formally presents to him at a feast for the Quillers Society held in her own lodge. He does not partake of the feast but leaves with the robe on a horse which has been staked outside the lodge by his mother-in-law as a gift for him. From this time on, the mother-in-law–son-in-law tabu is set aside for them.

This road is not open to many Cheyennes. It is a class privilege and a high achievement that may be grasped only by those who have shown the best character—the young man who has shown himself worthy in all areas, the woman of good family whose personal excellence is shown by her membership in the Quillers. Apparently, the fear of misbehavior and trouble that the existence of the tabu implies is adequately dissipated in a feeling of assurance that these two will not misbehave. The possibility of setting it aside shows also that the Cheyennes look upon the mother-in-law tabu as something onerous but necessary for the ordinary man.

A Cheyenne father-in-law may speak to his son-in-law, but he should not try to boss him. The young man's attitude is one of reserved respect.

Tylor long ago demonstrated that the forms of parent-in-law avoidance are correlated to the patterns of residence. Avoidance of the mother-in-law by a man is more common where uxorilocal residence (near the bride's parents) is the custom. A woman avoids her father-in-law more commonly where virilocal residence (near the groom's parents) is the mode. Since the Cheyenne normally are uxorilocal, we would expect the avoidance rules to be less stringent, if not entirely absent, in the case of a woman and her father-in-law. Such is, indeed, the case. A daughter-in-law must show respect and reserve in her associations with her husband's father, but both are allowed to speak to each other and to be in the same lodge together.

Because there is no need for inhibition of sexual impulses between a woman and her husband's mother, they may associate together freely, although the younger woman should behave with deference, "in the best way," as one Cheyenne put it to Eggan (Eggan 1955:55).

Parent-in-law and child-in-law relations are psychologically softened through the attitudes associated with kinship terminology. Son-in-law and daughter-in-law are both referred to by the grandchild term, *nixa*. Thus, they are brought within the speaker's kindred and closely linked by more than in-law bonds. The younger people refer to their parents-in-law by special terms of relationship which are derived from the words for grandparents but are nonetheless different. They express an impulse to fuse the older in-laws in the speaker's kindred while yet giving cultural recognition to the fact that they do after all belong to different kindred.

In sum, the Cheyennes do much to emphasize identity with families to which they are linked through marriage. They formally differentiated customary attitudes and behavior toward the different categories of affinal relatives in accordance with the functional requirements and variations allowed with respect to incest prohibitions and sexual repression, the maintenance of authority in the older generations, preferential marriage possibilities, and residence.

THE KINDRED

The Cheyenne kindred weaves its individual families into a finely knit cooperative body within which personal relations are carefully defined. For the Cheyennes, the kindred is more important than the inner circle of parents and children (Petter 1915:464). The kindred is not essentially a residential group. Potentially, it consists of all those persons who can be identified as relatives, whether through the father's or the mother's side. The kindred is bilateral. There are no lineages or clans in Cheyenne society.

The kindred is not a tightly organized group. The boundaries of its membership are not clearcut, because although all identifiable relatives are kin, not all are necessarily involved as members of any given person's kindred. The real kindred is made up of those relatives who actually help and support each other in such matters as food gathering and the collection of wedding gifts or the quantities of food and presents which must be given away when one of its members is elevated to a chieftainship or has pledged one of the sacred ceremonies.

Some kindreds are imbued with strong family feeling, and strive for public recognition. They engage the loyalty and energies of large numbers of kinsmen. Others lack pride and drive. They may have few active members because of losses through war and disease—or through lack of interest.

THE BAND AND CAMP

As the individual conjugal and composite families are the basic units within the kindred, the kindred is the basic unit within the band. Bands are made up of more or less closely related kindreds which customarily camp together. Camps are temporary settlements of widely varying size and composition. A single family, living alone, forms a camp. A single kindred, living by itself, forms a camp. Several related kindreds, living together, form a band camp. All the Cheyenne bands, gathered together for one of the Great Ceremonies or on a tribal warpath, form a tribal camp.

During most of the year, the Cheyennes live in widely scattered band camps wherever adequate forage for their horses is available and hunters may cover a wider range in search of game. The tribal camps are of brief duration, Lasting from mid-June through late summer, allowing enough time for an Arrow Renewal, Sun Dance, or Animal Dance, followed by a tribal buffalo hunt. The great tribal gatherings are occasions of tremendous social excitement and fun, but they are possible only so long as the buffalo herds are concentrated in large numbers. When the summer grasses turn from green to dried-up brown, and the bison herds begin to disperse, the Cheyennes find that they must also break up into more mobile and widely dispersed band encampments.

A Cheyenne is said to belong for life to the band in which his or her mother was living at the time she gave birth. The mother might well belong to another band altogether. Band identity is primarily explicitly residential with implicit kinship undertones, since bands are mostly composed of closely related kindreds. People who happen to live in the same *camp* may marry, so long as they are not recognized as members of the same kindred and do not belong by name to the same band.

The leaders of the band are the outstanding heads of the several kindred who make up the band. They may or may not be tribal chieftains or chiefs of one of the military societies. The head chief of a large band is almost certain to be a tribal chief, a member of the Council of Forty-four (see Chapter 5).

There are ten main Cheyenne bands, as follows:

1. Eaters, *omisis.* The Eaters say they got their name because their ancestors were such great hunters that they always had plenty of food. Other Cheyennes say it is because they will eat anything. The Eaters are the largest Cheyenne band and live in the north.

2. Burnt Aorta, *heviqsnipahis.* This name is believed to have originated in a past emergency situation in which a roasted aorta from the heart of a buffalo was used as a tobacco pipe. The women of this band have the habit of sitting with their feet to the left. All other Cheyenne women sit with their feet on the right.

3. Hair Rope Men, *hevatanui.* While other Cheyenne use rawhide ropes, this band customarily makes its ropes of twisted hair. The Hair Rope Men have been the leaders in the migration from the Black Hills into the southern plains.

4. Scabby, *oivimana.* Originally a kindred within the Hair Rope band, their headman, according to one account, developed a skin infection from using a mangy buffalo hide as a saddle blanket. Others in the family got the affliction from him.

5. Ridge Men, *isiometannui.* Another offshoot of the Hair Rope Men, who developed a preference for living in the "ridge country" at the head of the Smoky Hill River in Colorado.

6. Prognathous Jaws, *oktouna*. Distinguished by its practice of a dance, preliminary to going on the warpath, known as the Deer Dance.

7. Poor, *haunowa*. Origin of the name unknown.

8. Sutai. The band derived from the Sutai tribe that joined up with the Cheyenne late in the eighteenth century.

9. Sioux-eaters (Those Who Eat with the Sioux), *wutapiu*. The name of this band is the Siouxan word for Eaters. It originates from the incorporation of a Sioux group into the Cheyenne tribe at some time in the past.

10. Grey Hair, *masikota*. Also called Flexed Legs. There is said to be a large proportion of grey-haired children in this band.

During the latter part of the climax period, between 1837 and 1849, the Grey Hair band suffered two devastating tragedies which resulted in its absorption into one of the military societies, the Dog Soldiers.

In the first instance, Porcupine Bear, headchief of the Dog Soldiers, got involved in a drunken brawl in which he stabbed another Cheyenne, Little Creek, and then called on half a dozen of his kinsmen to join in the killing, which they did. All seven were exiled, along with their families. They were "out of the tribe." The next year, however, they successfully ambushed and annihilated a Kiowa hunting party of thirty people. From then on they developed such an impressive war record that other Dog Soldiers began to leave their band camps to live with the fierce exiles. Then, in 1849, cholera all but wiped out three bands in the south. The survivors of the Grey Hair band, unable any longer to protect themselves, joined Porcupine Bear's band of exiles and became Dog Soldiers. In a short time thereafter, all the Dog Soldiers left their kindred camps and moved in with Porcupine Bear's group. So the Dog Soldiers became a distinct band, and as we shall see later on (pp. 113–114), a third division of the tribe.

Other kindreds that are accustomed to camp on occasion by themselves apart from the main band of which they are members tend to form what might be recognized as embryo bands. Because these groups often have their own names, some early writers confused them with bands. Such groups are the Bear People, *nakoimana*, the White Cunning, *wokpotsis*—a reputedly quarrelsome group, hard to get along with—and the Northward Facing, *notamin*. The Shy People, *tatoimana*, originated when their family headman, Buffalo Chief, was exiled for killing two fellow tribesmen on different occasions. A number of his kindred followed him into exile and became markedly bashful and diffident when they met up with other Cheyennes.[1]

Finally, it is interesting to note in the names of the Cheyenne bands a total absence of any totemic identification with plants or animals. The names are nicknames, pure and simple. They do, however, reveal the important point that a society's culture is not a homogeneous leaven; subgroups have their subcultures. Bands retain their distinctive identity within the whole by persistently maintaining their own unique customs in some areas of daily living.

It is also worth noting that almost all of the Cheyenne emphasis in the building of mythological accounts of the origins of their institutions is focused on the tribal structure and not on the bands. The elaborate culture-hero cycles of the adventures and innovations of Sweet Medicine and Erect Horns explain

[1] Although this event occurred some hundred and seventy years ago, these people still live as an identifiable group in one corner of the Tongue River Indian Reservation in Montana. Contemporary Cheyenne say they still tend to keep to themselves.

and justify the Medicine Arrow complex, Sun Dance, and military societies. Another myth accounts in detail for the formation of the tribal council. On the other hand, what Malinowski calls "the charters of institutions" are un-formulated in the case of Cheyenne bands. The legends that ascribe the origins of band names are trivial and trite, often ambiguous and uncertain.

4 / The military and Robe Quillers societies

Cutting across the kindreds and bands are the sodalities, or clubs, of the warriors (the Dog Soldiers are a later exception). While hunting is a male activity woven into the interests of the family, fighting is an activity institutionalized in the organization of the military societies. The interests of these societies are individual and tribal rather than kin based.

The societies are not organized companies of the order of colonial militia in the early days of American settlement. They are, in their way, somewhat more comparable to local American Legion or V.F.W. posts—social and civic organizations mainly centered on the common experience of the members as warriors, with rituals glorifying and enhancing that experience, and with duties and services performed on behalf of the community at large.

The idea of the military societies is attributed to a mythological female founder of the Cheyenne governmental structure (see Chapter 5); Sweet Medicine is said to have given them their distinguishing insignia and rituals.

The five original military associations are the Fox, Elk (or Hoof Rattle), Shield, Dog, and Bowstring (or Contrary). In the nineteenth century, after the annihilation of all the Bowstrings by the Kiowas and Comanches in 1836, Owl Friend started a new warriors' club, the Wolf (or Owl Friend's Bowstring), as the result of a vision experienced when starving and freezing on a journey north. The Northern Crazy Dogs is the seventh club, a contrary association also patterned on the Bowstring idea and probably influenced in part by the Crow, Hidatsa, or Mandan Crazy-Dogs-Wishing-to-Die (see Lowie 1935:331–334).

In many tribal cultures, especially in Africa and Melanesia, men's clubs are age graded. Although this is true of the warrior societies of the sedentary village tribes of the northern Plains Indians, the societies of the Cheyennes, in common with the majority of Plains tribes, are ungraded. This means that the boys of a certain age do not join the lowest ranking club as a body and then progressively move up the ladder of clubs as they get older. When a Cheyenne boy is ready to go to war, he may join any club of his choosing. It is often that of his father or older brother, but by no means necessarily so. He may shift his membership later on, but it is most rare for him to do so. No one club is higher in status than another, although the popularity and prestige of the societies do shift from time to time. All the fraternities are fundamentally alike in their internal organization and activities; the differences are in their paraphernalia, dress, dances, and songs.

Each club has four officers or leaders. The leaders are the main war chiefs of the tribe, although any competent man may organize and lead a war party. The two head chiefs, who are the ritual leaders, sit at the back of the lodge when the club is meeting. The other two sit on either side of the door and serve as messengers—one might even say "ambassadors"—to the Council of Forty-four and the other military societies whenever a big issue is being discussed within the camp. These two are the bravest men in the society. They hold the post of honor at the door because when the camp is pitched tipi to tipi in expectation of an enemy attack, they hold the open gap in the circle against all assault.

Five of the seven associations also have four virgin daughters of tribal chiefs as maids of honor to participate in their ceremonies and to sit in the midst of the circle of war chiefs when they meet in common council. Select girls of "the very best families" who exemplify the Cheyenne ideal of chastity and perfect conduct are thus held up for others to emulate. Womanhood, though it is denied direct access to power and authority, receives high deference and social reward. All the members of a society call their four maids by the kin term "sister," and they may never marry one of their own maidens. Should one of these girls defile her chastity before she marries, it will bring bad luck to the warriors of her club. The Dog and Contrary Soldiers claim that they do not have any maids of honor because they do not dare run the risk of the girls making a slip.

Two of the concise descriptions given by Dorsey provide a sample of the features that characterize the different societies.

The Elk (Hoof-Rattle) society has over . . . one hundred warriors . . . and four Cheyenne maidens. There is a keeper of the drums and a keeper of the elk antler emblem, which is formed like a rattlesnake. Two of the bravest men carry spears with crooks at one end, the wood of the handle being bent around in a semicircumference. These two spears are wrapped as far as the points with otter skin. The shaft is further ornamented with two bands of otter skin about two feet apart, with four pendants of eagle feathers attached to each band for ornamentation. The spears are about eight feet long. All of the other warriors carry straight spears with points, wrapped with otter skin which has been dressed on the outside. Each warrior carries a rattle. This rattle is a stick about one foot long, covered with tanned buckskin, to which are sewed or tied several dry dew-claws of elk, deer, or antelope. The keeper of the elk horn is the leader in the dancing and singing. The elk antler used by these warriors is real. It is straight and has a body about two inches thick and about eighteen inches long. It has a head and a tail. It is fashioned like a snake. On the top of the snake's back are grooves cut about half an inch apart. When used for singing and dancing they put one end of this antler snake on top of a piece of rawhide and hold the snake's tail in the left hand and with the right hand they hold the shin bone of an antelope and rub it backwards and forwards over the snake's back, thus producing a loud, shrill sound like that of some animal. They have four sacred songs, four war songs, and about two hundred dance songs. One hundred or more warriors sing in unison with the time of the rubbing on the elk antler, thus making themselves heard for a long distance. According to the teachings of the great Prophet this antler was used to charm the buffalo. Whenever the tribe desired large herds of buffalo, elk, or deer to come near their camp the warriors would come together and chew the herb medicine used in all the sacred arrow ceremonies and blow it upon the elk antler to make it effective. Then the keeper would hold the snake effigy by the tail and draw the scapula toward himself so that the motion was made from the head to the tail. Having four times made this motion the buffalo and deer would be charmed and come to them. All the antelope and deer thus affected were killed and their dew-claws taken for making rattles for the warriors.

Aside from the rattles, spears, bows and arrows, individuals satisfy their own desires in the matter of dress. All the warriors of the various societies hold as sacred the elk antler. When dancing, the Hoof-Rattlers hold their spears in one hand their body erect. They jump up and down, keeping time with the singing and rattling.

The Fox or Coyote society derives its name from the fact that its members imitate the coyote in their power of endurance, cunning and activity. They outstrip their fellow-tribesmen in running long distances, playing games, etc. There are about one hundred and fifty warriors in this society, and a head chief, who carries a coyote hide with the hair left on. The society regards this hide as sacred. Having put their medicine on the coyote hide as well as on themselves, these warriors feel light, and can endure and can run a long distance without stopping. The society has a rattle keeper, who carries a red-painted gourd with stones inside to make the rattling. In old times this rattle was made out of buffalo hide, but lately the gourd has taken its place. This rattle is used to mark time in the dancing and singing, and its keeper is the leader in the dancing and singing, and he knows all the songs. The society has four sacred songs, part of which relate to the coyote; four war songs, and about three hundred dance songs.

When these warriors have a four days' dance they put up their lodge either in the center or in front of the camp-circle, and, just within the interior of the lodge the coyote hide is placed so that its head is directed toward the entrance. The chief with his assistants sit back of the coyote hide. When in view, this coyote hide is placed in front of the chiefs in the council circle. The four maidens who are admitted to this society sit in front of the chiefs. Two of the warriors carry a spear about an inch and a half wide. Between its ends is stretched a string, which gives the spear the form of a bow. Several kinds of feathers hang from the spear, and it has a sharp point. The other warriors carry straight spears. Each warrior has two eagle feathers stuck vertically in his scalplock, and carries a bow and arrows. All members of the socety dress alike. Their bodies and upper parts of their arms and legs are painted yellow, while the lower arms and legs are painted black. On the breast of each warrior, suspended by means of a string about the neck, is a crescent-shaped, black-painted piece of hide. The two eagle feathers in the hair are always worn and the spear is always carried in their hand when they are not abroad. When dancing, these warriors jump up and down rapidly, keeping time to the rapid and ever-increasing time of the music. The four maidens, who are daughters of chiefs, decorate their dress with elk teeth. Their faces are painted yellow and they wear two eagle-feathers upright in their hair.

In the past, the warriors of this society had their hair roached over the top from front to back to represent a scalplock, the sides of the head being shorn of hair. All members of the other societies wore their hair long. The coyote hide is the emblem of this society, for in a similar skin the great Prophet brought the medicine-arrows to the tribe. The coyote was the animal that the great Spirit sent to wander over the earth, and he was one of the animals that, in early time, talked to men (Dorsey 1905:I, 18–20).

The military societies have important auxiliary activities, such as policing the great tribal ceremonies (as already discussed), policing the tribal hunts, and working with the tribal council in making and enforcing law and government decisions.

Among the Cheyenne women there is but one organization, the exclusive and sacred society of the Robe Quillers. It is described in detail on page 68.

5 / The council of forty-four

The keystone of the Cheyenne social structure is the tribal council of forty-four peace chiefs. War may be a major concern of the Cheyennes and defense against the hostile Crow and Pawnee a major problem of survival, yet clearly the Cheyennes sense that a more fundamental problem is the danger of distintegration through internal dissension and aggressive impulses of Cheyenne against Cheyenne. Hence, the supreme constitutional authority of the tribe lies not in the hands of aggressive war leaders but under the control of even-tempered peace chiefs. All the peace chiefs are proven warriors, but when a chief of a military association is raised to the rank of peace chief, he must resign his post in the military society. He retains his membership, but not his position as war chief. The fundamental separation of civil and military powers, with the supremacy of the civil, which is characteristic of so many American Indian tribes and is written into the Constitution of the United States, is most explicit in the unwritten constitution of the Cheyenne nation.

A Cheyenne peace chief is chosen for a definite term of office—ten years—and ritually inducted as a member of the council. Each chief is a representative of his band and he is always a headman of an extended family. He is first and foremost, however, a "protector of the people," a "father" to each and every member of the tribe, and is addressed as such.

The chiefs are ordinarily beyond fighting age and usually hold back from battles, even when a Cheyenne village is attacked; but if the warriors are routed, the chiefs may go out as a body to try to turn back the enemy.

The personal requirements for a tribal chief, reiterated again and again by the Cheyennes, are an even-tempered good nature, energy, wisdom, kindliness, concern for the well-being of others, courage, generosity, and altruism. These traits express the epitome of the Cheyenne ideal personality. In specific behavior this means that a tribal chief gives constantly to the poor. "Whatever you ask of a chief, he gives it to you. If someone wants to borrow something of a chief, he gives it to that person outright."

"This is the first time since I have become a big [tribal] chief that I have happened upon such a poor man," announced High Backed Wolf after he had found Pawnee, who had been stripped and beaten by the Bowstring Soldiers for his crimes: "now I am going to outfit him." "Now I am going to help you out," he addressed Pawnee, after giving him a stiff lecture on proper Cheyenne behavior. "That is what I am here for, because I am a chief of the people. Here are your clothes. Outside are three horses. You may take your choice! Here is a mountain lion skin. I used to wear this in the parades. Now

I give it to you." To these things he also added a six-shooter (Llewellyn and Hoebel 1941:8). Such is the conduct of a chief.

Where ordinary men customarily accept damages when their wives run off with another man, a tribal chief refuses the pipe, horse, and gifts sent by the correspondent; acceptance implies that he nourishes a grievance that must be salved. Instead, he summons his soldier society to his own lodge and ritually smokes his own pipe with them. Nothing is said about the matter, but everyone understands the chief to signify that the affair is formally closed.

When Arapaho Chief was having a scalp shirt made, word was brought to him that his wife had run off with another man. He merely filled his pipe and passed it to the other men, saying he had no fault to find with her. (It is also clear that his wife knew it was perfectly safe to run away—especially when such a sacred thing as a scalp shirt was occupying her husband.) Chiefs, when such an advantage is taken of them, sometimes show their superiority to the indignity by remarking most casually, "A dog has pissed on my tipi." Men who do not have faith in their ability to control their feelings under extreme provocation refuse to accept a chieftaincy. When Little Wolf indicated he intended to name Sun Road as his successor as the Sweet Medicine Chief, in 1892, Sun Road refused, saying, "When a dog is running after a bitch in heat—if my wife is chased by another man, I might weaken and open my mouth. Then it would be well if another had the medicine and not I."

As Grinnell sums it up,

> A good chief gave his whole heart and his whole mind to the work of helping his people, and strove for their welfare with an earnestness and a devotion rarely equaled by the rulers of other men. Such thought for his fellows was not without its influence on the man himself; after a time the spirit of goodwill which animated him became reflected in his countenance, so that as he grew old such a chief often came to have a most benevolent and kindly expression. Yet, though simple, honest, generous, tenderhearted, and often merry and jolly, when occasion demanded he could be stern, severe, and inflexible of purpose. . . . They were like the conventional notion of Indians in nothing save in the color of their skin. True friends, delightful companions, wise counselors, they were men whose attitude toward their fellows we might all emulate. (Grinnell 1923:I, 336–337).

Such is the stuff the responsible leaders of the Cheyenne people are made of.

The charter of the institution of chieftainship and its organization in the Council of Forty-four is sacred. Sweet Medicine gave the people the Sacred Arrows and many other customs and institutions; Erect Horns brought them the Sun Dance and Animal Dance by way of the Sutai. But the mythological origin of the tribal council antedates all of these. Mooney (1907:371) cites a Cheyenne myth attributing the creation of the tribal council to a captive woman. Her husband had been a chief in her former tribe and she taught the Cheyennes its governmental organization. Grinnell (1923:I, 345) records a version in which a Cheyenne girl is taken captive by the Assiniboines. After a number of years she returns to the Cheyennes and tells them how the Assiniboines govern themselves; the Cheyennes, who are impressed with her account, adopt the Assiniboine system. The fact is, however, that the Assiniboines never had a tribal council anything like that of the Cheyennes.

The fullest recorded version of the origin myth of the Cheyenne Council of Forty-four is that recited to me by Black Wolf in 1936.

I once asked Elk River, when he was an old man, about that question. "Now we have chiefs," I said to him. "I wonder how we got those chiefs. Can you tell me? And how did we come to get the law against killing our own people?" This was many years ago and there were many people in the lodge when Elk River gave his reply.

"Yes," Elk River answered, "that was a long time ago, many years before our time, that this thing of which I shall tell took place."

This is what Elk River told.

People used to wander about the country in those days. There was one old man among them who took his family away from the main band to camp out alone. He stayed out here with them—his wife, his daughter, and a small son—for a long time, until one day he killed his wife and deserted his motherless children.

The orphan children wandered alone about the countryside seeking their tribesmen and shelter. At last they spied the main camp of their people in the distance. The first lodge they came to was that of an old woman of whom they asked news of their father. The old woman did not answer, but went to the lodge of an old man who was a camp crier to tell him that the children of Bull Looks Back had returned to the camp seeking after their father. This old man went out and announced the news to all the camp.

Bull Looks Back was right there among the people. When he heard the news he ran crying to the announcer, "Those monstrous children of mine killed their own mother out there and have eaten her flesh. That is why I left them. Tell the people that even though they are my own offspring, I say they should be staked to the ground and abandoned."

The camp crier repeated all that Bull Looks Back had said. "In the morning we must tie them to the ground and move camp as early as we can. We must not leave a living thing with them, not even dogs."

That night the people prepared green rawhide in rope lengths. The next morning they tied the boy and the girl to stakes driven in the ground and waited, sitting watching, until the thongs had shrunken tight and firm. Then the camp was moved.

[At this point the train of the narrative was broken when Black Wolf was asked whether a soldier society had carried out the deed. In response he gave the polite rebuke, "No, I asked Elk River that same question. 'I am telling the story,' he said. 'I'll come to that.' "]

There was one great, black dog. Maybe it had pups. At any rate, it had packed some stuff, meat and sinew, into a hole near the camp site. Toward evening the hapless siblings saw the dog coming up to them. It wriggled and scratched as a dog does and then went right to work chewing on the rope which bound the girl's wrists until they came free. The girl then untied her brother. They followed the dog to its hole in the creek bank, where it crawled in, and when it came out again it was dragging dried meat and some tools. They all ate and sat there.

During the night someone walked up to them, but the sister did not look up, for her head was hung in sorrow. This person addressed her little brother.

"Over there you will see a wikiup and an arbor. Go to it!"

"Sister," the little boy cried, "Look over there!"

"It will do me no good to look," she murmured. "They have been telling lies about us. This person has not come here to speak the truth."

"Look anyhow," the boy insisted.

So she raised her head, and she saw it was true.

Then the stranger spoke again. "In the morning—at daylight—a herd of buffalo will come. Have your sister look at them."

At daylight the buffalo came as the stranger had said. "My sister, look on those buffalo," the boy cried in delight.

"That herd won't die if I do look at them," she morosely replied.

Even so, she had medicine power from the man who had been there, though she did not know it. She looked, and at her glance all the buffalo fell dead! After that the boy and girl went to the wikiup.

A bear and a mountain lion were living there. Three beds were made up in the hut, so the boy and girl took the extra one.

Again the strange visitor appeared before the outcasts. He spoke to the boy as before. "Tell your sister she must butcher all those buffalo. She must look after all the meat and take care of all the fat. A big crow will come to one of these trees. When she has done her butchering she must put some kidney fat in the branches for it. That will be on the third day."

In the end, when the girl had finished her butchering, a crow flew down and looked at them. The sister spoke to it, because she now believed in the stranger. "Here, come get this fat. Fly with it straight to our people's camp. Fly right through the opening [in the camp circle]. Fly low about the circle. Then drop this in the center before the lodges. Tell those people it is from the children they left on the prairie to die."

When the people saw this, and understood the crow to mean that the two children had plenty of meat, they made ready to move the camp back to them, because they had been unable to find game for some time.

The boy and girl heard a man come singing. He was singing Elk songs.

"That is my father," the girl told the lion and the bear. "Do not harm him until he has eaten, but when he leaves this lodge, take him."

When the father came in, he was given the place at the back of the lodge. The girl sent word to the approaching people not to move in too close to her.

"I shall see you tomorrow," was her order.

When her father finished eating, the lion and the bear killed him for her.

She now sent for the men, and the women too, because she had cooked up a lot of food. When they had eaten she spoke to the men.

"Tomorrow you move down on this flat and put yourselves in a nice circle. We are going to make chiefs. You people know I have been accused of killing my mother. That is not true. Now, however, I have killed my father through animals. We shall make chiefs, and hereafter we shall make a rule that if anyone kills a fellow tribesman he shall be ordered out of the camp for from one to five years. Whatever the people decide."

When they had arranged the camp circle they took two big lodges and made one in the center. She asked them to move five other tipis into the space within the circle. These were put in the medicine wheel arrangement. When everything was finished she packed a large bundle and walked around the circle to enter it before the big lodge. First, she took some dirt from the north side of the lodge. Carefully patting it, she arranged it in a mound in the center of a cleared space. It represented the world. Next she set up five sticks representing the men she would choose as head chiefs. She filled her pipe. She held it to each stick, showing the people what would be expected of them.

"You will have to swear," she said. "You will have to take an oath that you will be honest and care for all the tribe."

Following the instructions she gave out, her brother purified himself in the smudge of the sweet medicine grass. Now she told him to go out to walk four times around the camp.

"When you go out you have a starting place. Go around until you come back to it. Do this four times," she ordered.

He had already been told what men to select. After the four circumambulations he sought out the first man, leading him into the lodge. Then the other four were brought in like manner.

When they were seated, the sister told them everything. She had all she needed in that bundle. She told them she was going to make them chiefs to rule the camp. And this is what she said.

"You have seen me put up five sticks here. You shall have to do this to the others who come after you. Now you five men are to be the chiefs of the entire tribe. You must rule the people. When the tribe comes to renew the chiefs you must put up these five sticks again. If anyone of you still lives, and the people want him again, then you must call him in to take his old place."

Now she has finished telling them. [Changes of tense are the narrator's.] She is going to swear them in. She is holding the pipe herself, in both hands with the stem out. They smoked. The pipe is smoked for peace. That was done so that if some persons ever used strong words to the chiefs, they would have strong hearts and not get angry. The sweet grass was used on all of them.

Then the big crowd came in. Enough more were in the lodge to make forty-four men. She did the same to each of the rest of them. When this was done she told them to pick two men to sit on each side of the entrance.

"Some day you will have a lodge of your own," she informed them. "Then you can use these two. They can cook for you, or you can send them out on errands. They shall be your servants and messengers."

These two could not be of the five.

"Every ten years you must renew the chiefs. But each time keep five of the old ones," the maid continued.

She had a parfleche for the stuff they used in the ritual.

"When you move camp," she exhorted them in closing, "keep out in front of the people. Stop and rest four times with it [the chiefs' bundle] on the way" (Llewellyn and Hoebel 1941: 69–73).

After she had made all the chiefs, she took out five bones, just as many as these five chiefs. "Now you can make soldiers troops. You may call them what you want. You could call one Elks." Later on, Sweet Medicine made the dress of the soldiers.

"When you people move camp, leave me here. Every four years, you come back to this place where I will be."

Next she made a medicine wheel and a buffalo horn which she gave to the old woman to whose lodge she had first come. "On your travels you will sometimes go hungry. If you use these, it will make the chiefs think of their duty."

Later that year the people were hungry. Then the old woman remembered what had been told her. She told a young man she was going to try it out. She had him go collect some rose berries. She cooked them up. That night she had him stay in her lodge to help her. They built an incense smudge of cedar and coals over which they purified her pipe, wheel, and buffalo horn. She sang four holy songs all through. When each was done, she ritually smoked the pipe. Then it was daylight.

She told the boy to go up a hill to scout. "We shall see if she told us the truth."

From the top of the hill he spied buffalo in the distance. He came back and reported the news.

"Good," she said. "Go get Howling Wolf." He was one of the new door chiefs.

Howling Wolf sent out a crier to tell the people, and they went out on the hunt right from the camp, the buffalo were so close.

After they had the hunt and everyone had his meat, they asked the boy how he knew there were buffalo out there; they had not seen any for several days.

"My grandmother did that," he told them. "She fixed up her lodge and did the ceremony the way that girl told her. The woman we left behind in her camp and were not to see until next fall, she had the power to do this."

After that, a bunch of chiefs went into the old woman, asking her how she knew the buffalo were going to be there that morning.

She replied, "I was told how to do this by the girl who was left behind in camp. She told me how to do it. I am only supposed to do this once in a while when there is great need. If you chiefs will fill up the pipe and bring it in here, I'll tell you how to do it. Take out the tenderloin from a buffalo. Dry it well. Pound it up very fine. Keep this handy."

The camp had been moving for some time; they were running out of food again. One of the chiefs asked the young man to ask his grandmother if it would be the right time to ask for more food. His grandmother told him, "Tell the chiefs to come to my lodge late this evening just before sunset. All who are coming must enter at the same time." She told him what they must bring—that tenderloin powder, rose haws, and pomme blanche (prairie potato). When they got there, the pipe was the first to go in. She had the lodge all fixed; the Earth and everything were ready.

One of the chiefs did the speaking, begging her to show them how her power went. The old woman told them, "I am not the one who is doing this. I am only performing as *she* told me. She sent us out on the move to keep going until fall. When we get back to her camp, my job is done. I am teaching you this now in case anything might happen to me!"

They laid out the horn. Then she took the pipe, pointing it in the five directions. They smoked.

Then she spoke, "I am not supposed to do this as long as there is a single buffalo for the hunters to take. I could not do this on my own. This is not just my doings. It is given to me to do for the people."

She then made the remark, "I'll still use this young man as my helper."

"Bring me a coal and place it here."

On this she put some sweet grass.

"Now I am going to sing four songs. At the end, we shall smoke. You chiefs have the pipe ready before me."

She sang the first song and then lit the pipe, praying as she pointed it to the five directions. When all had smoked, the boy had to get a fresh coal.

They refilled the pipe, and she sang the second song. At the end, all smoked again.

They did this for each song. It took them all night. Daylight was breaking as the old woman finished the fourth song.

When the song was done, she addressed them, "Now that grandson of mine, my helper; he usually does these things for me, but you chiefs, you are the ones who want to know how this is done. Is there any young man among you who is willing to go out and see?"

Howling Wolf was in there. He was the one they chose.

She spoke to Howling Wolf as follows, "Now I want you to do just as my grandson has done. Get a coal and put it before me with the sweet grass!"

She smoked all those ritual things in the incense. The last thing was done. The ceremony was finished. She was talking all the time to this man, instructing him. "When you go out the tipi door, turn south and then go west. When you see the buffalo, keep going and turn back; come in the north side of the lodge."

He made his trip quite a way out. He came back and reported buffalo moving toward the camp making quite a noise. The chiefs sent him right out to tell the same old man to cry the news to the whole camp. When it was announced, all the men got ready for the hunt. After the chase, they all came back with meat. They just had all the meat they could handle.

It was announced through the camp that they were going to help the old woman out. They all thought that she was a great woman—a medicine woman. They brought her meat and clothes.

Then they started back to find the holy girl who had given them these things. It was fall when they got there. She told her little brother to tell the chiefs to arrange the camp in a circle as before. The old woman and her helper seemed to be the only two who could go into the girl's lodge. The girl told her, "Now when you go back to the camp, tell the people they must put up a dance. They must build a great skunk (bonfire). One bunch of solders must dance. Then another, until all have danced."

The soldiers were going to select one of the chiefs to be out in front. Certain persons were selected to do the choosing. Four men from each soldier society and four from the council of chiefs were chosen. When the warriors were all in line with these men out in front, this holy woman emerged from her lodge, standing before them.

She spoke to the four chiefs, "These men your warriors have selected are your soldier chiefs. You must now fill your pipe and swear them in. They are here to protect you. You are to look out for the people. When there is fighting or work to be done, these soldier chiefs are here to do it."

"Now you may wander about the country again, wherever you wish to go. But do not forget this one thing, ever. Every now and then repeat this ceremony. Your four head chiefs are to remind the soldier chiefs of their duty."

"And never come back to this spot again. I shall leave here and you shall never more see me. And another thing—do not abuse the dog. It was the dog who saved my life and taught me these things."

"In your wanderings, the time will come when you will meet a great holy man [Sweet Medicine]. He will change your way of life. He will tell you where to go. He will give you your home."

"My brother and I will leave this earth. We may go up into the heavens. Yet I shall always be working for the people. I may be a star." Her name was Mukije, Short Woman.

Thus ended the story as told by Elk River, who was born about 1810 and died in 1908 (Hoebel n.d.).

There are a number of aspects to this myth. First, it established the tribal council as supernaturally vested and as the oldest of the existing institutions of the formal social structure, thus the ultimate authority. Second, the act of perfidy and abuse of children by a parent, and the killing of the parent in revenge are examples of what may happen within the society if there are no strong regulations to prevent it—an anarchy the Cheyennes feel must ever be guarded against. Third, in times of personal stress and despair, supernatural animals appear to give power and instruction in how to achieve one's goals. Fourth, the military societies were given their governmental functions after the tribal council was formed and are explicitly made subordinate to the council in these matters. Fifth, it is made clear that Sweet Medicine and his innovations are a later event in Cheyenne mythological history. Sixth, ritual acts have a compulsive effect in producing desired results.

Let us now turn to the actual organization of the council. Its presiding officer, the head priest-chief of the tribe, is the Sweet Medicine Chief. He holds the Sweet Medicine Bundle, a small ritual package of sweet grass passed from one office holder to the next. He is taught the rituals of his office by his predecessor. When the council is in session, he sits at the west side of the Chief's Lodge. The spot at which he sits is called "the center of the universe," *heum* (the zenith, the above), and this is the title the Sweet Medicine Chief carries. In front of him, in the lodge floor, is the usual smoothed-out circle of earth, representing the world. Around it are placed, upright in the ground, the five sticks representing the five medicine chiefs, Heum and his four associates.

These four also represent cosmic spiritual beings, and each of them must have pledged or acted as instructor in either the Arrow Renewal, Crazy Animal Dance, or Sun Dance at least four times. The one who sits in the southeast side of the lodge circle is called *hunsowun* (an untranslatable holy name). He represents the Spirit Who Rules the Summer. He is always an Animal Dance priest. Across from him, in the northeast position, sits the representative of the *maijunemistist* (the Big Holy People—those who know everything, those who taught Sweet Medicine and Erect Horns; they are associated with the Northern Lights). This direction and its associated chief is also called *maxkeometaneo* (Where the Food Comes From). In the southwest position sits *niomataneo* (an untranslatable holy name), who is associated with *aijunt'tsemiats*[se] (the Spirit Who Rules the Ages). He is always a Wolf Club Ceremony priest. Opposite him, at the northwestern spot, sits the *no'tam* (another untranslatable holy name), who represents *paiwustannewus*[te] (the Spirit Who Gives Good Health).

The mystic symbolism of the dependence of the Cheyenne on the supernatural world is thus woven into the very nucleus of their governmental structure. At its heart, in their belief, the council is not just a body of their wisest men, but a council of men in empathy with the spiritual forces that dominate all life—beneficient forces from which come all good things the Cheyenne heart desires, forces that respond to their hopes and needs so long as the compulsive ritual acts are faithfully repeated.

The five sacred chiefs are always chosen from among those who have already served a full term of office as an ordinary chief. A sacred chief may succeed himself for a second term, or he may step down to an ordinary chieftainship if he feels he does not want to carry the responsibility of the office any longer. At the end of his term as one of the five, Brave Wolf got up and told the other chiefs how he had served the people as chief, how he had been through many ceremonies for them, how he now wanted to be relieved. They agreed, but "held him in the lodge"—that is, named him to one of the thirty-nine lesser positions. Under no circumstances may a tribal chief be impeached or deposed during his ten-year tenure of office, not even for murder. When Little Wolf killed Starving Elk in 1879 (see Llewellyn and Hoebel 1941: 82–84 for the details of the case) he was then the Sweet Medicine Chief. Although he went into exile, he still remained chief, and when the council convened for the next renewal it could not proceed until Little Wolf had been induced to come in and officiate over the rituals. "I've done wrong," he told them. "I killed a man, and I don't think I ought to sit with the chiefs."

"We need you," was the council's reply. "We can't proceed without you." But he was not retained as a member of the council. Grasshopper replaced him as the last head chief of the Northern Cheyennes. When Grasshopper died, the Sweet Medicine Bundle was gone. The Cheyennes believed it had been contaminated by contact with Little Wolf's body, and so Grasshopper buried it.

A hundred years earlier, before 1800, another chief had killed a tribesman and was banished. People talked against him, saying, "We will take him out of his place." "But," in the words of Calf Woman, "the Indian law stopped it . . . he was still a chief, though all by himself." After two years, he was allowed to rejoin the tribe and resume his functions as a chief.

Bear Runs Out, as a young chief, accepted a horse as damages from a young man he had seen flirting with his wife. For this unchiefly conduct he was censured, and when his term was up, he was let out of the council. After another ten-year term had passed, and he was a mature man of more sober judgment, he was renamed to the council because "he was a great protector of the people in war."

Each chief, if he is still alive at the end of his term, chooses his own successor from within his own band. Thus every band normally has at least four representatives on the council. Although the office is not hereditary, a man frequently chooses his own son to succeed him—if the son measures up to the qualification for chieftainship. The office is always looked upon as a grave responsibility and not as a political plum. It brings respect and honor, but nothing else. There are no economic advantages; quite to the contrary, being a chief means having a drain on one's resources. "Among those qualified for the position of chief, there was no strife as to who should secure it, no 'wire-pulling' or intrigue" (Grinnell 1923:1, 341). Refusal to accept a nomination brings bad luck. Big Head, for example, refused a chieftainship in the middle of the last century. He was killed in his next battle.

The Chiefs' Renewal, or the naming and investiture of a new council, is almost as solemn and important a ritual undertaking as the Medicine Arrow Renewal. The Chiefs' Lodge is placed in the center of the camp circle, with the Arrow Keeper's and Buffalo Hat Keeper's lodges also in the open space within the circle. Four days of secret world-revitalization rites precede the actual selection and investiture of the new council. At the end, each new chief gives his predecessor a gift. All the chiefs come forth to be viewed by the people, and the ceremony is followed by festive feasts in honor of the chiefs and the giving of many presents by the new chiefs, especially to poor people.

Cheyenne government, it may be seen, is highly democratic and representative of the people's concerns. Each band has an approximately equal number of members on the council, and the ratio of forty-four chiefs for no more than four thousand Cheyennes is better than one representative to one hundred citizens.

The council is a serenely deliberative body. As described by Grinnell,

> At the meetings of the council of chiefs, questions of interest to the tribe were considered. Concerning minor matters, one of the principal chiefs was likely to express his opinion, and, if supported by another principal chief, the council assented without debate. Questions of greater importance, such as moving the camp when buffalo could not be found, of undertaking a tribal war, or of seeking an alliance with other tribes for the purpose of proceeding to war against a common enemy, were discussed at great length, the deliberations perhaps extending over several meetings. In such debates the talking was done chiefly by the older men—those of greatest experience—yet after the elders had expressed their views, middle-aged men expressed theirs, and even younger men might speak a few words, suggesting a different point of view, or giving new reasons for or against a certain course.
>
> Such councils were conducted with much form and with a degree of courtesy that could hardly be exceeded. Usually the subject of the council was known in advance and to some extent had been discussed. When all the chiefs were present, a few minutes of silence ensued, then one of the older men arose and introduced the subject at issue. His remarks were followed by a brief silence for consideration, when another old man followed him and the discussion continued. Sometimes there were wide differences of opinion among the men, yet each was listened to gravely and with respect, and no matter how earnest the debate might become, no man

ever interrupted a speaker, nor did anything like wrangling occur. (Grinnell 1923:I, 338–339)

Although only the chiefs themselves and a few other older men may be in the lodge, most such meetings take place in the summer when the tipi sides are rolled up, and a large public audience sits around outside listening to the discussions. As soon as a decision is reached, a camp crier rides through the camp circle announcing the decision of the council. The chiefs discuss the reasons for the action with their own kindred and bands, so that everyone is well informed as to what is to be done—and why.

In addition to treating such matters as camp moving and tribal war policy (as against individual raiding expeditions), the council also acts as a judicial body in cases involving a criminal act (see Chapter 6). In governmental affairs, it further serves as executive and legislative authority over the military societies, which act as the administrative police branch. In matters of war and peace, however, the warrior groups have an active say in the decision-making process. They can, in fact, ignore and thereby nullify the ruling of the council in matters in which they are vitally concerned. The council, although it has the constitutional authority to act on its own, takes realistic cognizance of this hard fact.

Thus when the Kiowas and Comanches, hereditary enemies of the Cheyennes, made a proffer of peace to Seven Bulls and his war party of eight men (they were brought together by an Arapaho host in whose camp the Cheyennes and their enemies accidentally came together as guests), Seven Bulls replied,

> Friend, you know we are not chiefs. We cannot smoke with these men, nor make peace with them. We have no authority; we can only carry the message. I have listened to what you say and tomorrow with my party I will start back to our Cheyenne village, and will carry this word to our chiefs. They must decide what shall be done. We are young men; we cannot say anything; but we will take your message back to the chiefs.

He was as good as his word. The council was assembled the day after his return and he and his companions were invited in to report their message. Prolonged debate brought no agreement. Then the proposal was made to put the question to the Dog Soldiers. This was accepted and the two Door Chiefs of the Dog Soldiers, White Antelope and Little Old Man,[1] were sent for. After a briefing, High Backed Wolf, the presiding officer of the council, told them, "Now, my friends, you go and assemble your Dog Soldiers. Tell them about this matter and talk it over among them. Let us know what you think of it. Tell us what you think is best to be done."

When the Dog Soldiers had convened in their lodge, White Antelope described the problem in full, concluding his remarks with, "The chiefs are leaving this matter to us, because we are the strongest of the military groups. It is my own thoughts that our chiefs are in favor of making peace. What do you all think about it?"

The Dogs unanimously agreed to leave the decision to White Antelope and Little Old Man, who were their two bravest leaders.

They declared for peace with the Kiowas and Comanches. On their return

---

[1] Porcupine Bear, the leading head chief of the Dog Soldiers, was in exile, it will be remembered (p. 38, above).

to the Council Lodge, this was the decision they recommended on behalf of the Dogs. Thereupon, the chiefs all arose and thanked them gravely. This done, they sent the crier about the camp to announce that the council had decided peace would be made with their erstwhile enemies (Grinnell 1915:60–66). Thus began in 1840 an alliance of friendship that was never violated. The matter began with the good offices of a third party, the Arapaho, and was carried with due respect for authority to the council. The council licked the thorny problem of possible defiance of its authority by delegating the power to act to the key group in question. The Dogs responded by recognizing the validity of the chiefs' inclinations. The Dogs forestalled dissension by delegating the decision to their two greatest warriors and then announced it to the council as a unanimous opinion. The council discharged the Dog Soldiers with thanks and asserted its paramount authority in announcing the decision as its own. Here is true parliamentary statecraft, a formal structure kept functionally flexible so that the structure remains intact and yet expediently bends when necessary to achieve an important immediate goal not otherwise likely to be realized.

6 / Law and justice

Law may or may not be a matter of government, although it is always a matter of political organization—the system of regulation of relations between groups or members of different groups within the society at large. Public law—the body of legal rules governing conduct held to be of such concern to the whole society that it is administered by public officials in the name of, and on behalf of, the society as an entity—is an aspect of government. Private law—the body of legal rules governing conduct deemed to be of immediate concern to the injured party but indirectly recognized as of concern to the society at large—although not necessarily an aspect of government, is always an important part of political organization. In many primitive law systems, private law predominates over public law; not so, in the case of the Cheyennes.

The Cheyenne concern with the threat of internal disruption and their compensatory drive toward tribal supremacy and unity on all crucial matters have resulted in the centralization of legal control in the tribal council and the military societies. The bulk of Cheyenne law is public law: the heart of Cheyenne law focuses on murder and the control of the communal hunt; disputes over property are rare; adultery and wife stealing rarer. Violence of Cheyenne against Cheyenne is the great challenge to the Cheyenne system of social control, and the existence of this danger stems from the fact that Cheyenne basic values are contradictory at certain points. On the one hand, the individual is trained and encouraged to be militarily aggressive. He is publicly rewarded with many ego-satisfying reinforcements for sterling performance on the battlefield. But—as will be demonstrated in Chapter 11—his training leads to strong repression in the development of many phases of his personality. He is taught to be competitive in the achievement of war status and horse-stealing reputation. At the same time, he must repressively control his sex drives, and he is trained in social altruism and mild demeanor within the camp. It is therefore not surprising that violent emotions often break through the bonds of self-restraint in homicidal assaults on fellow tribesmen. In our special study of Cheyenne law (Llewellyn and Hoebel 1941) we obtained case records of sixteen intratribal killings over the four decades from 1835 to 1879.

As an operating system, Cheyenne law is remarkable for the degree of juristic skill that is manifest in it. By juristic skill we mean the creation and utilization of legal forms and processes that efficiently and effectively solve the problems posed to the law and in such a way that the basic values and purposes of the society are realized and not frustrated by rigid legalism. Juristic skill implies the ability to define relations between persons, to allocate authority, and to clear up conflicts of interests (trouble cases) in ways that effectively reduce internal social tensions and promote individual well-being and the maintenance of the group as a group. We have commented on this outstanding quality of the Cheyennes: "It is not merely that we find neat juristic work. It is that the *generality* of the Cheyennes, not alone the 'lawyers' or the 'great lawyers' among them (whom they show no signs of having recognized as such) worked out their nice cases with an intuitive juristic precision which among us marks a judge as good; that the *generality* among them produced indeed a large percentage of work on a level of which our rarer and greater jurists could be proud" (Llewellyn and Hoebel 1941:312–313).

The greatest of Cheyenne governmental and legal achievements has been the absolute and total elimination of feud. The feudistic tendency is the bane of primitive social systems generally. Feud means internal war, civil strife between the kinship groups within the society; feud means either the absence of law, or else the breakdown of legal machinery. The absence of feud among the Cheyenne is in part a result of the system of bilateral kindreds at the bottom of the social structure. In such a system the strands of kinship are generally diffused throughout the society in a more multiple way than is the case in unilaterally organized social structures. This factor, however, is not in itself a wholly efficient cause for the absence of feuding, for other bilateral societies are known to be plagued by feud. What, then, are the additional elements that have been worked into their culture by the Cheyennes?

We are already familiar with the ritual devices used to emphasize tribal unity and the importance of "Cheyenneness" above band identity. We have seen, further, how it is impressed upon the chiefs that denegation of self-interest is in harmony with a sense of obligation to the well-being of all the tribe. This emphasis, too, contributes to the reduction of the feud potential. But, in addition, there are specific concepts related to the killing of a fellow tribesman and specific mechanisms for dealing with homicide when it does occur.

The first of these is purely mystic and relates to the major tribal fetish, the Four Sacred Arrows. A murderer becomes personally polluted, and specks of blood contaminate the feathers of the Arrows. The very word for murder is *he'joxones,* "putrid." A Cheyenne who kills a fellow Cheyenne rots internally. His body gives off a fetid odor, a symbolic stigma of personal disintegration, which contrition may stay, but for which there is no cure. The smell is offensive to other Cheyennes, who will never again take food from a bowl used by the killer. Nor will they smoke a pipe that has touched his lips. They fear personal contamination with his "leprous" affliction. This means that the person who has become so un-Cheyenne as to fly in the face of the greatest of Cheyenne injunctions is cut off from participation in the symbolic acts of mutuality—eating from a common bowl and smoking the ritual pipe. With this alienation goes the loss of many civil privileges and the cooperative assistance of one's fellows outside of one's own family. The basic penalty for murder is therefore a lifetime of partial social ostracism.

On the legal level, the ostracism takes the form of immediate exile imposed by the Tribal Council sitting as a judicial body. The sentence of exile is enforced, if need be, by the military societies. The rationalization of the banishment is that the murderer's stink is noisome to the buffalo. As long as an unatoned murderer is with the tribe, "game shuns the territory; it makes the tribe lonesome." Therefore, the murderer must leave.

Banishment is not in itself enough, however. His act has disrupted the fabric of tribal life. Symbolically, this is expressed in the soiling of the Arrows, the allegorical identity of the tribe itself. As long as the Arrows remain polluted, bad luck is believed to dog the tribe. Not only does the spectre of starvation threaten, but there can be no success in war or any other enterprise. The earth is disjointed and the tribe out of harmony with it. The Arrow Renewal is the means of righting the situation. The oneness of the tribe is reasserted in the required presence at the ceremony of every family—save those of murderers. The renewed earth, effected by the rites in the Lone Tipi, is fresh and unsullied, once again free of the stain of killing.

Such a concept of the effect of homicide within the tribe completely precludes the possibility of feud. Feud would merely compound the sin, making disaster for the tribe complete. Nor is there any possibility of a death penalty for the crime. Extrusion and ostracism are eminently effective. In the same vein, no steps are taken to compensate the bereaved kin group for the death of its member. The offense is against the well-being of all the people; hence concern of a mere kinship group is as nothing.

Yet it is contrary to Cheyenne principles to so ostracize a man forever. The Cheyennes cherish the individual personality. They value individualism, asking only that the individual never place himself above the tribal interest. They therefore work always toward reform and individual rehabilitation. For them, the law is corrective; it is never employed as a vindictively punitive measure. Punishment, in their view, need go no further than is necessary to make the individual see the right. Once they are convinced the knave is reformed, they move smoothly to reincorporate him into the community. The case of Pawnee, cited above, is but one example of this. So, also, with the murderer. After a period of years—three, five, or ten—his banishment may be commuted. At this point the feelings of the relatives of his victim are taken into consideration, for they must consent to the commutation.

For example: Cries Yia Eya was banished for killing Chief Eagle in a drunken brawl. He had not been seen for three years, when he turned up with a horse laden with tobacco. Stopping outside the camp, he had a friend lead the horse in to the chiefs along with the message, "I am begging to come home."

The chiefs called in the soldier chiefs and divided the tobacco among them, saying, "Now we want you soldiers to decide if you think we should accept his request. If you decide that we should let him return, then it is up to you to convince his family that it is all right."

The soldier chiefs convened their societies in their separate lodges. The door servants kept passing back and forth between them, reporting the trend of opinion. At last one man proposed, "I think it is all right. I believe the stink has blown from him. Let him return!" This view won out.

Then the father of Chief Eagle was sent for. "Soldiers," he replied, "I shall listen to you. Let him return! But if that man comes back, I want never to hear his voice raised against another person. If he does, we come together."

Cries Yia Eya, according to Calf Woman, had always been a mean, unpopular person, but after he came back to the camp he was always good to the people (Llewellyn and Hoebel 1941:12–13).

In one tragic incident, recorded by Grinnell, there was no reconciliation; rather, a tribal "execution" of a two-time killer was engineered. This case of a murderer irretrievably beyond the pale began in 1854, when Walking Coyote killed a chief of the Fox Soldiers, White Horse, for taking his wife. He had some cause for his extreme action in that White Horse had not sent him the customary pipe and gift. Another Cheyenne, called Winnebago, pledged the Arrow Renewal, but then overreached himself by preempting the wife that White Horse had originally taken. Walking Coyote retaliated by forcibly taking one of Winnebago's other wives while her husband was away in the north. Upon his return, Winnebago shot and killed Walking Coyote within his lodge.

The Arrows were renewed, and Winnebago left the tribe. But eight years later, he was back again when a kinsman of White Horse raised a dispute with him over ownership of a horse. In the brawling that followed, he killed this kinsman in self-defense. The Arrows were renewed again, and Winnebago went to live with the Arapahos.

Rising Fire, a member of the same kindred as Winnebago's two victims, was goaded into a grudge feeling against Winnebago by skillfully planted, malicious gossip. Winnebago was lured into an ambush by the members of his own Dog Society, who, inviting him into the Cheyenne camp for a feast, led him past the lodge of Rising Sun, who shot and killed him (Grinnell 1923:I, 350–353).

This case shows that residual urges to kin blood revenge are still present; that woman stealing, with arrogance, can occur—and is so outrageous in the view of the individual Cheyenne as to lead to utterly reckless behavior. And finally, that when banishment does not effect reformation (even though Winnebago was sorely provoked in his second killing), banishment is not enough; the death penalty can be imposed, but indirectly and by crafty expediency on the part of the soldiers. For there are no formal institutional patterns in Cheyenne culture to deal with this kind of marginal irresponsibility. It happened only once in all known Cheyenne history.

Suicide is homicide—a self-killing. We have already seen how brothers plan to get themselves killed when sisters flout their authority. But they let the enemy do the killing and their post-mortem reward is glory, not disapproval. Direct suicide is a protest act of girls and women, and for both, the protest is an expression of grievance within the conjugal family. The social reaction follows two lines. A woman who hangs herself because her husband brings home a second wife is said to be foolish for killing herself over such a little thing. Second wives are normal. In the public view there is no valid protest, and nothing is done about it. On the other hand, there are the two cases of girls who killed themselves after they had been scolded and whipped by their mothers. One had eloped against her mother's wishes. The other had left her husband and returned to her parents' lodge. She angered her mother by joining in a young people's dance, which was an unseemly thing to do. Each of the mothers was mobbed, and beaten, and then exiled for causing her daughter's death. And in both instances, the Arrows were renewed for the killing (Llewellyn and Hoebel 1941:160–161).

Outrageous conduct leading to a protest suicide *is* tantamount to killing that person. Such conduct is *de jure* homicide. Banishment and tribal expiation must follow.

Abortion, too, is homicide within the meaning of Cheyenne law. An un-born fetus has legal personality as a Cheyenne. Its death through abortion brings the full penalty of exile on its mother (Llewellyn and Hoebel 1941:118–119).

If the first concern of Cheyenne law is to nullify the dangers in intratribal killing, the second is to insure the security of the basic food supply through the communal hunt. From the time of the performance of the great ceremo-nies to the splitting up of the tribe at the end of the summer, no man or private group of men may hunt alone. During the early summer months the bison are gathered in massive herds, but distances between herds may be great. A single hunter can stampede thousands of bison and spoil the hunt for the whole tribe. To prevent this, the rules are clear, activity is rigidly policed, and violations are summarily and vigorously punished. The police for any given summer are ordinarily the members of the soldier society of the pledger of the tribal ritual with which the summer has opened. If for any reason there is a question as to who should police the hunt, the Council of Forty-four names the fraternity which is to have the job.

In a typical case the tribe was moving up the Rosebud River in Montana looking for buffalo in the direction of the Big Horn Mountains. All the hunters were in a line with the Shield Soldiers to restrain them until the sig-nal was given, for the scouts had reported buffalo. Just as the line came over a protecting ridge down wind from the buffalo, two men were seen riding in among the herd. At an order from the chief, the Shield Soldiers charged down on them. Little Old Man shouted that any who failed or hesitated to beat the miscreants would be beaten themselves. The first to reach the spot killed the two hunters' horses. As each soldier reached the criminals, he lashed them with his whip. Their guns were smashed.

The offenders were sons of a Dakota who had been living with the Cheyennes for some time. The father said to his sons, "Now you have done wrong. You failed to obey the law of this tribe. You went out alone and you did not give the other people a chance."

The Shield Soldier chiefs took up the lecturing. The boys did not try to defend themselves, so the chiefs relented. They called on their men to con-sider the plight of the two delinquents, without horses or weapons. "What do you men want to do about it?" Two offered to give them horses. A third gave them two guns. All the others said, "Good!"

Then it was noticed that five or six members of the troop were not present. They were searched for and spotted chasing buffalo. A chief gave the order to charge and whip them but not to kill their horses. Big Footed Bull, who was one of the miscreants, saw them coming. He took off his Hudson Bay blanket and spread it on the ground before his companions and himself. The soldiers rode around them in two columns, dismounted, and cut the blankets into strips to wear as part of their dance costumes. They did not whip the men, but they did cut an ear off each of their horses (Llewellyn and Hoebel 1941:112–113).

In good Cheyenne manner, the first violators were severely punished—and then immediately rehabilitated as soon as the soldiers sensed they had learned their lesson. As for their duty-shirking comrades, they, too, quickly signal-ized their error by offering the blanket. They were spared physical punish-ment but their one-eared horses and the spectacle of the other members of their troop dancing with their blanket strips was an unpleasant public reminder for a long time to come.

Even the tipi of a person suspected of secretly hunting may be searched by the soldiers. Man-Lying-On-His-Back-With-His-Legs-Flexed accidentally came upon a herd when the no-hunting rule was in force. He killed and butchered just one cow. He was seen and informed on. The Shield Soldiers went to his lodge and cut a gash down the back of it. He sat inside, saying nothing. By this they knew he was guilty, whereupon his whole lodge was destroyed. On another occasion, someone carried tales on Low Forehead. He was innocent, and rushed out holding up his hands in protest when the Fox Soldiers arrived at his lodge. Their chiefs entered and searched it. Finding nothing, they left him unmolested.

Such great tribal figures as Little Wolf and Old Bear have received punishment in their time for violating the hunting rules. On this one point the Cheyennes are most inflexible.

A special problem case was once raised in this connection by Sticks-Everything-Under-His-Belt. He announced ahead of time that he was going out hunting for himself. A special council of the Forty-four and all the military societies was called to deal with this crisis, for Sticks-Everything-Under-His-Belt had made it clear that he meant to act as though he were not a member of the tribe. The formal ruling was: So be it. No one might help him thereafter in any way. All the privileges of being a Cheyenne were to be denied him. But, the chiefs left the door open for his return. If anyone did help him, that person would have to give a Sun Dance. This was posed as a penalty. But giving a Sun Dance is an honor and, as we have seen, an occasion of tribal integration.

Sticks-Everything-Under-His-Belt went into mourning all alone. He was strictly shunned for several years. In the end, his sister's husband announced to the chiefs that he was bringing him back into the tribe, if the chiefs would agree. They thanked him, saying, "We are very glad you are going to bring back this man. However, let him remember that he will be bound by whatever rules the soldiers lay down for the tribe. He may not say he is outside of them. He has been out of the tribe for a long time. If he remembers these things, he may come back."

Then Sticks-Everything-Under-His-Belt was invited to appear before the council. The pipe was passed and smoked by all. Then he declared himself. "From now on," he asseverated, "I am going to run with the tribe. Everything the people say, I shall stay right by it. My brother-in-law has done a great thing. He is going to punish himself in the Sun Dance to bring me back. He won't do it alone, for I am going in too."

All the chiefs had to dance, too, under the conditions stated by the pledger. The dance, which took place near what is now Sheridan, Wyoming, was a memorable one. The spot is still remembered as Where-the-Chiefs-Starved-Themselves (Llewellyn and Hoebel 1941:9–12).

It is in the facing up to new crisis situations such as this that the Cheyennes show their real legal genius and their capacity for treating their culture as a working instrument for the realization of social ends.

The introduction of horses, of course, has posed new problems. Theft within the tribe has never been a troublesome matter, for a person receives as a gift anything he asks for, and those who are well off are always giving to their less fortunate fellows. Horses are given away to honor many special occasions. Nonetheless, by 1850 the taking of horses without asking had become a sore point with some owners. The issue was finally brought to a head by Wolf-Lies-Down, whose horse was "borrowed" in his absence. The borrower had left his bow and an arrow in Wolf-Lies-Down's lodge as identification and surety, but after a year he had still not returned the horse. Wolf-Lies-Down put the matter before his military society, the Elk Soldiers. They sent a messenger off to the band where the borrower was staying in order to bring him in. When he did arrive, he was leading the borrowed horse, plus another one. He explained he was sorry he was gone longer than expected and that he was giving Wolf-Lies-Down the second horse as well as the one that belonged to him.

Wolf-Lies-Down said that was fine and from now on he and the other man would be bosom friends (that is, formal "brothers"). The Elks then wound up the whole matter by declaring that it would be that way between the Elks and the society of the borrower. "Our society and his shall be comrades. Whenever one of us has a present to give, we shall give it to a member of his soldier society."

But there was more. "Now we shall make a new rule. There shall be no more borrowing of horses without asking. If any man takes another's goods without asking, we will go over and get them back for him. More than that, if the taker tries to keep them, we will give him a whipping" (Llewellyn and Hoebel 1941:127–128).

The incident illustrates four points: 1) law-making and law-enforcement powers, independent of the tribal council, on the part of the military societies; 2) a neat cleaning up of the immediate sore spot; 3) a formalization of friendship between the individuals who were on the point of becoming potential enemies, with multiple reinforcement of the positive relations by virtue of the entire fraternity taking the same step; and 4) the laying down of a clear legal norm for the future, with the penalty stated for an errant "borrower." This became a rule for the whole tribe.

A short time later an incorrigible juvenile delinquent named Pawnee learned to his rue that the rule was to be enforced. He was a notorious horse "borrower" and troublemaker. When he ignored the new law, the Bowstring Soldiers took after him and tracked him down three days out on the trail. They beat him unmercifully, destroyed his clothing and saddle, ruined his gun and everything else he had with him. Alone on the prairie, he was preparing to die, when High Backed Wolf found and rehabilitated him (see above, pp. 43–44).

The Cheyennes are also capable of rejecting proposed new legal norms when they are assessed as potentially dangerous. This happened when Walking Rabbit tried to introduce the Comanche practice of permitting a man to take a woman away from another man by making her a member of a war party. When Walking Rabbit turned up with a stolen wife, the raid was immediately halted and the warriors went into council to consider what should be done about the situation. They flatly rejected the proposition that the wife absconder and his companion should go along with them. Walking Rabbit was sent back home—but again with the cooperative softening of the blow; everyone promised to give Walking Rabbit arrows to send the aggrieved husband. Several promised horses. So it was done. Walking Rabbit's father had already settled the case, when his rash son got back with the girl. When the raiders returned, he proposed that they give the horses and arrows to her kin. This they did in a grand gesture. Her relatives gathered exchange goods. "The war party was called together once more; to them this stuff was given. It was a great thing for the people to talk about. It was the first and last time a woman was sent home on enemy horses the day they came in" (Llewellyn and Hoebel 1941:13–14).

In this and other new matters of immediate urgency, the fighting men, either as a military society or as an *ad hoc* war party, can "legislate" law, which on the basis of its fundamental soundness finds general acceptance. Such matters need not necessarily go to the council when they do not involve a direct challenge to rules already established under council jurisdiction. Social solidarity and cultural flexibility are attained in a variety of ways.

C. Subsistence and War

7 / Hunting and gathering

The homeland of the Cheyennes is the high portion of the Great Plains. It is a vast, grasslands area naturally devoid of trees except along the watercourses and the foothills of the mountains. Its elevation ranges from three to five thousand feet, except in the mountainous portions to the west. Climatically, the entire country is subhumid, the mean annual rainfall varying from only ten to twenty inches a year. A deficiency of water is in fact the distinguishing climatic characteristic. Most of the precipitation falls in the summer, often in the form of stupendous, crashing thunderstorms. The runoff is quick, except where water gathers in buffalo wallows, and the evaporation rate during the hot, dry days is high. The grass is of the short-grass variety. It grows luxuriantly in the late spring and early summer, and at that time the bison gather in immense herds. As summer progresses, the grass dries and becomes sparser; the herds break up into widely scattered foraging units. This is the essential ecological fact controlling the Cheyenne seasonal rhythm of tribal in-gathering and band dispersion.

In addition to facing the searing heat of the summer, the Indian must confront the winds. "The level surface and the absence of trees gives air currents free play. On the whole, the wind blows harder and more constantly on the Plains than it does in any other portion of the United States, save on the seashore" (Webb 1931:21). Of the summer winds Ward (1925:405) writes that their characteristics are "their intense heat and their extreme dryness." "Everything" notes Webb, "goes before the furnace blast. . . . A . . . common effect is that these hot winds render people irritable and incite nervousness [we wonder if Cheyenne breakthroughs of personal violence relate to this]. The throat and respiratory organs become dry, the lips crack, and the eyes smart and burn." It was under such conditions that Erect Horns went to the Sacred Mountain to learn how to bring forth the game and get rain and verdure from Thunder. Is it any wonder that Cheyenne ceremonies work constantly for world renewal, for the blessed conditions that prevail in the spring and early summer?

In the winter, people must contend with the wind in its opposite extreme in the form of either the "norther" or blizzard. The norther comes with little warning, "often accompanied by a solid sheet of black cloud and clouds of sand, and causes the thermometer to drop with incredible speed from twenty-five to fifty degrees." A personal account of an army wife en route to Fort Arbuckle in 1867 contains this description:

The second morning dawned mild and clear, almost summer-like—an ominous quiet soon to be broken by a sound like the roar of the ocean. A gust of wind almost blinded us with dust. The driver exclaimed in terror: "A norther." Hastily we lowered the ambulance curtains, adding buffalo robes as the cold increased to a bitterness that is indescribable. Soon a storm of snow like white sand is whirling all about us. Our mules should have dropped, had not their drivers run at their sides, beating them vigorously (Eastman 1935:23).

A wet norther is a blizzard, "a mad, rushing combination of wind and snow which neither man nor beast can face." But outface it with their primitive equipage the Cheyennes must—or go under.

The land of the Cheyennes is not a paradise. But, when at its benevolent best, it is a challenging land with the beautiful serenity of vast vistas and the "Big Sky"—a bountiful land of millions of bison and antelope easily taken when the season is right; a land of roots, seeds, and berries for those who know where to find them; a land where a person can get a full, satisfied belly on rich meat balanced with a variety of wild vegetables. But it is still a land where starvation is a spectre never far off, and cold, death, thirst, and maddening heat must be ever confronted. It is a land where people must hold together, or perish; where people must "know how," or soon be done in; where the Cheyennes have come to rely not only on technical skill but on mystique and compulsive ritual to bolster their sense of security and give them a faith which will engender courage.

WOMEN'S ACTIVITIES

Men and women cooperate to supply the food, but the division of labor is strict. Women are the vegetable gatherers. The dibble, or digging stick, is their basic tool. It was given by the Great Medicine Spirit and it figures in the ritual paraphernalia of the Sun Dance, for it has its sacred aspects. Cheyenne dibbles are of two types. The short kind has a knob at one end and is pushed under the desired root by pressure against the stomach when the digger is down on both knees. The other kind is long, and used as a crowbar. The sharp ends are fire hardened.

Some eight or ten different wild roots are gathered, including the bulbs of several varieties of lilies. Most conspicuous of the tubers used is the well-known Indian turnip (*Psoralea lanceolata*), also known by the French name, *pomme blanche*. It is dug in the spring when still edible, and is sometimes eaten raw, but more commonly boiled. After cutting it into slices, the Cheyenne women dehydrate it by sun drying for year-long preservation. Dried slices are pulverized and used as a thickening for soup. It is a major source of starch. The "red turnip" (*Psoralea hypogeoe*) is smaller and more tasty, and a great favorite of the Cheyenne palate.

The fruit of the prickly pear cactus (*Optuna polyacantha*) is collected in parfleche bags, worked over with twig brooms to remove the spines, and finally picked clean by the women, who wear deerskin thimbles especially made for the purpose. The fruit is then split, the seeds removed, and the remainder sun dried. The product is added to meat stew and is also used as a soup thickener.

Milkweed buds, collected just before the flowers opens, are boiled in soup or stew. The "milk" of the plant is evaporated to make a favorite chewing gum.

Thistle (*Arsium edule*) stalks are peeled and eaten with great pleasure. [Old-time Cheyennes, in the 1930's, compared it with the banana as a delicacy.]

Many varieties of berries are collected by the women, but most common is the chokecherry (*Prunus melanocarpa*). The whole berry, including the pit, is pulped on stone mortars and made into sun-dried cakes. Mixed with dried, pounded meats, it produces the best pemmican.

Of the wild plants gathered by the women for their family larder, some sixteen varieties are fruits, eight or ten are roots, and a dozen to fifteen are vegetable stalks or buds. Many of them add variety to boiled meat dishes or nourishing quality to soups. The Cheyennes do not bake or fry breads made of plant flour.

Although root digging is a tiresome chore, the girls and women do not treat it as such. They leave the camp in the morning in small work parties without a male guard against enemy marauders. Their spirits are usually gay, for they look on the day's activity as an outing. Far out on the plains they scatter to their individual tasks, for the actual gathering requires no cooperative effort. When they come together in the late afternoon, they often react to the monotony of their work by gambling their roots against each other in a game of seeing who can throw her digging stick the farthest, or by throwing "dice" of buffalo metacarpals.

If it is *pomme blanche* they have been gathering, they excitedly anticipate the sport with the men that awaits them at the camp. The sport consists of the women making believe they are a war party and the men are their enemies. When not far from the camp, they arrange their roots in a row of piles and take their positions behind them, sitting down. Now one woman rises and signals with her blanket, letting out a great war whoop. In the camp the men start up, and other women rush out to see the fun. The young men grab scrubby old horses and lazy nags. Some snatch women's rawhides from under the pounding stones. Others already have imitation shields of willow twigs. Pounding away on their burlesque war steeds, whooping and hollering like mad, they charge down on the line of root diggers. These await them with ammunition of sticks and chips of dry buffalo manure which they let fly when the men are within range. The men dodge and twist; one who is hit is "wounded" and out of the game. Only one who has had a horse shot under him or has himself been wounded in war may dismount to snatch some roots, if he gets through the barrage unscathed. Others just mill around making a great to-do. When a few roots have at least been captured, the men withdraw to a hill to eat them and joke about their exploits and casualties while the women pick up their burdens and go on into the camp.

Sometimes the men plan a surprise attack during which, after counting a coup, they may make off with some roots. But if the women see them coming, they gather together behind a circle drawn in the ground with a digging stick. This represents a fortified camp, and no man may cross the line unless he has killed an enemy or counted coup within enemy breastworks. He who has done so dismounts after entering the circle, recites his coup, and exercises his privilege of helping himself to as many roots as he wishes to carry away. If there is no man in the party who qualifies for this deed, the women hoot and insult the men who presumed to attack them.

This horseplay reveals several things. In the first place, of course, it provides fun and sport after a day of monotonous work. But its special form is significant. It is clearly a vicarious release of suppressed sex antagonisms: the men attack the women, and the women dare them to do it. Yet the men are at the same time satirically burlesquing the pretensions of their own superiority to women—save for those few men who are sterling examples of Cheyenne success in warfare. The others are targets of ridicule and refuse hurled at them by taunting women.

Women also go out in foraging groups to gather wood for their fires. Except for collecting expeditions, however, most of a woman's work when the camp is not moving is in and about the lodge preparing food, dressing hides, sewing and decorating clothing, robes, and lodges. A good woman is cheerful, busy, and skillful. The raising and lowering of tipis is solely the job of women, and they do it with skill and speed. In the more permanent camps they excavate the floor of the tipi four or five inches, leaving a sod bench around the outer part to serve as a foundation for the beds. The bare floor is wetted and packed down. A lodge lining is tied part way up the poles and folded inward over the bench so that no draft blows under the tipi cover on the sleepers. With the help of her children, the lodge mistress gathers bundles of grass to lay on the bench as padding. Mats made of horizontal willow withes which are attached to tripods are raised between the ends of each sleeping place and covered with buffalo robes to form backrests. In well-provided lodges each person therefore has a comfortable chaise longue as well as a private bed. A couple of buffalo robes are enough to keep the sleepers warm and comfortable within the tipi no matter how cold it may be outside. The areas under the backrest tripods form cupboards for the storage of gear and the parfleches of dried food.

The basic household item of the woman is her stone maul—an oval river stone with pecked-out grooves on the short sides around which is fixed a supple willow withe firmly fastened with green rawhide. When dried out, the rawhide shrinks and holds the maul within the handle with the grip of a vise. With the maul she breaks up fuel, drives tipi pegs, and crushes large bones to be cooked in soup. With smaller handstones the housewife crushes her chokecherries and pulverizes her dried meat.

Every household has its complement of horn spoons. These are made by steaming or boiling the horns of buffalo or mountain sheep until pliable. Tortoise shell and wood are also sometimes used.

Prior to contact with white traders, the Cheyenne women produced a variety of pottery dishes for cooking and serving. Now these have been supplanted by trade goods. Crude wooden bowls and dishes continue to be used. For the carrying and storage of water, "Western" water bags are conveniently fashioned from buffalo pouches, bladders, or pericardia. The general name for water bags, *histaiwitsts* ("heart covering"), suggests the most ancient form.

Each woman has a tanning kit of four tools: a scraper, flesher, drawblade, and softening rope or buffalo scapula (shoulder blade). The scraper is a prepared flat, oval stone held in both hands and used to remove extraneous meat and fat from the inner surface of the hide. Metal scrapers supplied by traders are also used.

The flesher is a more delicate instrument. Shaped like an adze, it is made of an elkhorn handle bent at right angle, with a sharp chipped flint lashed across the short end. It is used to hack down the inner surface of the skin to get it to the right degree of thinness. Its proper use is a high skill, and a good fleshing tool is a cherished family heirloom. Grinnell acquired a flesher that had passed through the hands of five mothers and daughters (all known) and had been in continuous use for about a hundred and fifty years when he received it.

The drawblade is a slightly curved willow stick, into the concave side of which is glued a sharpened bone splinter. With the hide draped over an inclined pole, the woman worker shaves off the hair from the outer side of the skin.

Tanning calls for chemical applications; otherwise, the result is rawhide. Brains, liver, and soapweed provide the essentials of the working compound, which is mixed with grease to provide body. The stuff is well rubbed into both sides of the hide, which is then put to soak overnight. After drying in the sun, it is laboriously softened by being worked back and forth over a raw-hide rope or by being pulled through a hole in a buffalo shoulder blade fastened to a tree.

A small lodge requires eleven buffalo cowhides, thinned and tanned. A big lodge takes as many as twenty-one. A woman does all the work on her lodge skins up to the point of the rope- or blade-softening process. For this last step she invites in her friends and relatives—one for each hide—and gives them a big feast. Each one is then given a hide to take home to finish, with a rawhide rope to use for the work. Meanwhile, she has to split and make quantities of thread from the buffalo sinews she has been hoarding. Her next chore is the preparation of another great feast, for the process of cutting and sewing the lodge is an all-day sewing-bee to which all her friends will bring the hides she has parceled out to them. At daybreak she must first seek out a woman known as an expert lodge maker, to whom she supplies paint and a cutting knife. Before the guests arrive, the lodge maker fits the pieces and marks them for cutting. The sewers subsequently arrive for breakfast and work all day long, with a meal in the afternoon and a supper at night—this last after the lodge has been raised and stretched on its foundation. For her pains, the expert lodge maker receives a small present.

A new home is a great thing for all the tribe, and it is so recognized in a ritual of dedication. Except for the women working on it, no one may enter a new lodge until the bravest man available has counted coup on it and has entered, followed by other outstanding warriors. The women have completed a hard and great piece of work, and in this way the men give recognition to their achievement.

All clothing is also made by the women. Unfamiliar with the art of weaving, they tan the necessary skins and loosely tailor the garments for themselves, their men and children. Awls are made of ground-down bones (animal or fish), or thorns. These, with thread and decorative materials, are kept by each women in a hair-covered leather bag worn at her belt. Dresses are tubular sacks sewn together down the sides and reaching well below the knees. Short sleeves hang down from the shoulders.

Old-type moccasins are made of one piece, with the insole as a flap which is folded under and sewed along the outer edge. A durable rawhide sole is sewed on to this. The result is tough and comfortable footgear. Later types are constructed with a separate upper sewed onto a rawhide sole. They are adorned with porcupine-quill or trade-bead embroidery done in geometric patterns, or with little cone-shaped tinklers of tin, obtained from the white traders.

The essential garment of the male is the breechclout. Without it a man believes he will become unsexed, and so regards it as a magical protector of his virility. It is no more than a soft, square skin worn in front and suspended from a cord around the waist. In ceremony and many dances it is the sole garb. In summer, or on a raid, it may be all that is worn; there may be more, but never less.

In inclement weather, the men add leggings which cover the leg from moccasin top outside to the hip and inside to the crotch. Most of them have long fringes or a flap of deer skin on the outside below the knee; either way, walking makes quite a stir. Men's shirts are fashioned much like women's dresses, except that they reach no more than half-way to the knee and have full sleeves. A fully dressed man looks as though he is wearing trousers with a tunic, although the leggings do not, of course, make real pants. Shirts are highly decorated with quill embroidery, trade beads, or, in special cases, the scalps of enemies sewed along the seams of the sleeves. Buffalo robes round out the cold-weather garb of both sexes.

The quilling of robes is an extra, decorative flourish done as a vowed deed. It is a sacred occupation controlled by the Quillers' Society, mentioned earlier as an honored and exclusive group of select women. A woman or girl not a member of the society has to obtain the help and direction of one member as well as the assistance of the other members. The whole procedure of instruction is highly ritualistic and sacred. The neophyte must provide food and materials. Before the work begins, all the women recite the making of their best pieces—just as a warrior counts coup. An old male crier announces to the whole camp what is being done and publicly invites some poor person to come to see the girl who is going to decorate her first robe. For coming, the visitor receives the gift of a horse, and if he is a man, he rides it around the camp singing a song of praise extolling the giver. Two to four brave warriors are invited to the women's "coup counting," and when the women have told their quilling exploits, the men tell their great war deeds and dedicate the kettle of meat, which is offered to the spirits and divided among the women.

The sewing is done later. If a mistake is made, a warrior who has scalped an enemy must be sent for. He tells his coup and says, "And when I scalped him, this is how I did it," so cutting the misplaced quills loose.

When the Quillers are sewing the lodge decorations, the warriors may "attack" them in a very formal way. They choose a scout who at some time has been the first to spot the enemy, and he goes into the Quillers' lodge to see what they have to eat. He is followed by the bravest of all the men, who counts coup on the pot and is privileged to carry away the food without objection from the women.

MEN'S ACTIVITIES

While women gather vegetable foods and make the home and its accoutrements, men bring home the meat, make weapons, wage war, and perform the major part of the necessary rituals.

The Cheyenne men are almost exclusively big-game hunters. Bison stand out as their basic target with antelope next, then deer, elk, and wild sheep. Smaller game, such as wolves and foxes, are taken occasionally for their furs. Of their domesticated animals, the dog is a favorite delicacy reserved for feasts. "With us, a nice fat, boiled puppy dog is just like turkey at Thanksgiving with you," High Forehead used to say to me. Horsemeat is eaten, but not preferred. As a heritage from their days in the Woodlands, the Cheyennes (unlike most Plains tribes) also take fish.

A superficial paradox governs buffalo hunting. When buffalo are scarce, anyone may hunt when and as he pleases. When they are plentiful, the restrictions of the communal hunt come into force. The reasons for this are clear and simple: while scattered buffalo in small herds cannot be efficiently hunted by large groups, the massive early-summer herds, as already indicated, are best attacked by a closely working, cooperative group.

The communal buffalo hunt is a development stemming from the old-time antelope drive, which was a mystic procedure. Antelopes, as is well known, are the fleetest of animals, adapted to survival by speed of flight. They are at the same time, however, endowed with an odd sense of curiosity. They want to observe any unusual object and will, for instance, move toward a gently moving flag. It is this trait that the Cheyennes seized upon, magically elaborating their exploitation of it. In the nineteenth century, magical antelope surrounds (hunts) have become infrequent, but every now and then some medicine man puts one on. The basic pattern is not confined to the Cheyennes, but is widespread among Indians of the Plains, Great Basin, and Southwest (Underhill 1948:28–34).

The antelope shaman receives his power from Maiyun in a series of dreams. When he feels ready to put on a hunt, the news is passed by word of mouth rather than through a crier. This, and the fact that the shaman also lets it be known that no guns or ordinary weapons are to be used in the hunt, indicates that the pattern was set before the tribe established itself in the Plains, for the crier and gun are both culture traits acquired after the Cheyennes had migrated into the Plains.

As a first step, the shaman raises a small medicine tipi within which he performs an all-night ritual, the details of which are not known. At certain stages, the members of a military society beat on the lodge covering over four of the lodge poles which are mystically endowed. If the hunt is going to be successful, large quantities of antelope hair fall off the lodge covering.

The next morning, the shaman leads the people out toward where his power has told him the antelope will be. The hunters are on their fastest horses, but he is afoot. At the chosen spot, he selects two exemplary virgin girls. They must be good-tempered, or the antelope will be fractious and hard to control. They should also be plump, or the antelope will be skinny and stringy. Each is given a so-called antelope arrow: a wand with a medicine wheel at one end. The shaman has already used these to draw the antelope toward the spot. Each girl begins running outward on diverging, diagonal courses so that their paths begin to describe a wide V. Two young men, supposed to be their suitors, chase after them on the fastest and longest-winded horses available. The hunters on their horses tail out after them in two long lines.

As soon as the hunters are on their way, the remaining women and children form a circle at the foot of the V, with the shaman in the center. As the two leading young men pass the pair of girls, each takes one of the wands the girls have been carrying. They continue on the diverging line for a couple of miles, riding at a fast pace. Soon they are on both sides of an antelope herd, which, instead of running away, turns toward the shaman. The men with the wands then turn in and cross behind the herd, continuing to ride back outside the lines of hunters, who have followed them and entirely surrounded the herd. When the two reach the shaman, they return the wands. Down the V the antelope are driven at a fast pace, pell-mell into the circle of old men, women, and children, who with waving blankets close around them to form a human corral. Using his two wands as directional signals, the shaman makes the antelope rush around and around until they are utterly confused and exhausted. This is the drama that is reenacted in the Crazy Animal Dance. Then the people set upon the befuddled beasts and kill them with clubs. For his pains and skill the shaman receives all the tongues (a choice delicacy) and his choice of two antelope. The two girls and two young men make their choice next. After than, an even distribution is made among all the families.

William Bent, the trader, was with the Southern Cheyenne in 1858 when such a hunt was held under the direction of White Faced Bull. It was so successful that every one of six hundred Cheyenne lodges had an antelope, and Bent's wagon train had all it could use (Grinnell 1923:I, 288).

Other times, antelope are led and driven into a pit or over a bluff in the same way. Occasionally, the V is formed of brush piles behind which people hide until the antelope are between them.

The same technique is also applied to buffalo hunts. On one such occasion some enemy Shoshones turned up just after the hunt was completed. The Cheyennes attacked them in the ordinary battle manner, but afterwards thought it a shame that the Shoshones had not arrived a bit earlier. "We could then have sent those two girls around them and killed them all off just as we had the buffalo" (Hoebel n.d.).

For general purposes, the nonmagical hunt suffices in taking bison. They are not so skittish as the antelope, and the soldier-policed secular hunt is more usable as an everyday affair. In such hunts, when the charge is made, the hunter rides his horse up along the right side of a running beast and sends an arrow down and between its ribs. The horses are trained to follow tight beside the animal so that both the rider's hands are free to use the bow. Strong men sometimes shoot an arrow right through one bison and into another. If a spear is being used, it is driven down with the full force of both arms, between the ribs and into the heart. If a man is not good enough to do this, or conditions are not right, he thrusts for the kidneys, which are easier to reach. This does not bring such a quick kill, but it is a fatal wound with which a buffalo cannot run far. Lances and bows are preferred for large hunts even by those Cheyennes who possess guns, for many more animals can be killed this way; guns are too slow to reload for a man on horseback.

When the hunt is done, the men skin and butcher the take, loading it all on pack horses for the trip back to the camp where it is turned over to the women for cooking or cutting into thin slices which are hung on racks to sun dry. Later, the dried meat is shredded by pounding with the stone mauls and packed away as pemmican.

Deer and elk are taken by individual hunters who stalk them with bow and arrow, or ambush them from hiding places along their trails.

The large gray wolf is taken in pitfalls—deep holes dug wider at the bottom than at the top so that the wolf cannot jump out. A pole with bait at the center is staked across the hole, which is roofed over with split reeds covered with earth and grass. As the wolf moves out on to the mat to seize the bait, the whole covering gives way beneath him. He may then be shot in his prison.

Since foxes are too light to be taken this way, they are caught in deadfalls. In this type of trap two logs are arranged, one on the ground and another supported by a trigger above it. A little willow twig house, open at the deadfall end, is built over the baited trigger. Thus, the fox is forced to put his head under the fall-log if he is to get at the bait. A tug on the lure springs the trap; the log falls on his neck or back, killing or paralyzing him.

Eagles are not eaten but are highly prized for their feathers. They are caught by human hand and strangled. This is a crafty, ticklish undertaking, and one for specialists only—men who have eagle-catching power and knowledge of its associated rituals. Eagles have a wingspread up to seven feet and a beak as long as their heads. The trick is done from a pit-blind, which must be painstakingly prepared. The pit can be dug only when there are no eagles in the sky, and the dirt must be scattered a long way off, because eagles are far-sighted and cautious. Before digging the pit, the eagle catcher must sing his sacred eagle songs alone in his lodge all night long. His pit, which is just large enough for him to sit in, is roofed over with long grass through which are left a few spy holes. He deodorizes himself in a sweat bath and greases himself all over with eagle-grease paint. He enters the hole before daybreak, when the eagles cannot see him. Over his head a piece of fresh bait is tied firmly down. When an eagle settles down to tear at the bait, the hunter slowly slips his hands through the grass, grabs its legs and pulls it into the hole. The hunter is then in a 3-by-5 hole with a fighting, clawing eagle that he must strangle with a noose! The reward is considerable prestige and a good return in trade value: a horse for twenty or thirty feathers, for example. Eagle catching must be done in four-day stints (a ritual requirement). At the end, a ceremonial offering and apology are made to the dead eagles, followed by the hunter's taking four sweat baths to neutralize the sacred power worked up for use in the enterprise.

Turtles are taken from ponds and roasted or boiled in the shell for food.

When still in the lake country, the Cheyennes used to seine for fish, setting willow nets into which they drove the fish. Now they construct a fish weir in rivers under the supervision of a medicine man. The weir is a circle made of willow poles driven closely together into the bottom and lashed with rawhide. The weir is left alone at night for the fish to enter, while the medicine man in his lodge tries to draw them into the pen. During the next day, one man works with a long, narrow basket which is placed against an opening made in the downstream side of the weir. As the fish enter his basket, he removes them and tosses them up on the shore for the waiting people.

In summing up, we see that the Cheyennes provision themselves with a fair variety of food that gives a reasonably balanced diet in good times. Their techniques and skills are of a high order; they work together in smoothly cooperative teams for the common weal. Still, they live under feast-or-famine conditions, and famine is never forgotten. So uncertain is their food situation that, except for root- and berry-gathering activities, and the policed, secular buffalo hunts, ritual and supernatural power suffuse their undertakings. They are anything but improvident, and the drying power of the High Plains sun is constantly used to preserve meat and vegetables for leaner times. That the Cheyennes go to such lengths to preserve their food supply, despite the fact that it must all be packed along whenever they move, is indicative of their efforts to maintain their larder.

8 / Trade

It would be wrong to think of the Cheyennes, or almost any other North American Indians of the past several hundred years, as being self-sustaining hunters or gardeners. We have already seen how eagerly the Cheyenne reached out to draw La Salle with his trade goods to their villages. However, for the greater part of their known history the Cheyennes have not been as deeply involved in the fur trade as the tribes which keep a base on the Missouri River or the lakes and water routes of Canada. For one thing, they have never learned to trap beaver commercially. Instead, they have seized upon the newly introduced horse and moved farther into the west to escape, insofar as possible, the scourge of the Sioux and Assiniboine. Few traders followed them out into the plains until well into the 1800s. This is because they have found it too difficult to locate the nomadic bands in their wanderings over the vast grasslands. And, further, the Arikara and Sioux have blocked the traders from passing up the Missouri to establish direct trading relations with such tribes as the Cheyennes, Arapahos, and Crows. With hardheaded business sense, they have tried to exploit their own special position as hosts to the traders and as middlemen to the less favorably situated tribes. They have also attempted to limit the western tribes to as few guns as possible, thus controlling their ability to resist the raids of the Sioux in their westward press toward the Black Hills.

So, the Cheyennes continue their practice of making long trips back to the Missouri River villages, which have remained recognized market centers. The Cheyennes arrive with packhorses and travois loaded with dried buffalo meat, pemmican, and flour made of the dehydrated roots of the wild prairie turnip (*pomme blanche*). They also bring in their famous decorated robes, shirts, and leather pouches.

Everything that comes originally from animals is the product of the joint efforts of both men and women. The men hunt and kill. Their wives and sisters skin, tan, and decorate the hides. They also thin-slice and sun-dry the meat. It is the women who dig, dehydrate, and pulverize the turnip roots. Most of the hand labor that goes into the production of Cheyenne goods for the traders' market is that of the women. Among the Blackfoot, as Oscar Lewis (1942:38–40) has shown, this led to an increase of polygyny among the higher ranking men, and it may also have done so among the Cheyennes. Both Cheyenne men and women engage in the trading activities which take place at the Arikara villages.

The really big item in the trade between the Cheyennes and the Missouri

73

River tribes is the horse. In this traffic, the Cheyenne males are the chief middlemen. They acquire some horses in trade from the Arapaho and the Spanish settlers at Taos. Others they simply steal in raids on the Spanish New Mexican ranches, as well as the herds of the Crows, Comanches, Kiowas, and Utes. These horses they move to the markets of the northeastern plains. It is an easy, if dangerous, road to prosperity. All of these activities, both on the part of the women and the men, have obviously introduced many changes into the daily and seasonal lives of the Cheyennes.

In exchange for their productive and trading efforts, the Cheyennes enhance their diet with corn (maize), beans, squash, and tobacco, grown in surplus quantities by the village tribes specifically for the trade. From the Europeans and Americans, either directly or through the medium of the village Indians, they add sugar, molasses, wheat flour, eastern-grown tobacco, and whiskey. All of these are in a sense luxury foods, since the Cheyennes could readily survive without them. But life would not be so interesting. The same is true of the traders' colored cloth, beads, brass, jingle bells, silver jewelry, looking-glasses, and other tradeable merchandise, all of which add aesthetic pleasure but little, if any, productive effectiveness to the Cheyenne life style.

Important as the luxury items are to the Cheyennes, the driving force in motivating trade is utilitarian. Foremost is the gun and the powder and shot to go with it. The bow and arrow is still preferred for hunting, because it is more efficient at close range than the single-shot musket. But in war, the advantage goes to the side that is best armed with guns. Axes, hatchets, iron spearheads, arrowheads, and knives are desired by all Cheyennes for peaceful use as tools and for deadly use in hunt and battle. To the extent that it becomes available, metal replaces the chipped and ground stone artifacts of pre-European contact days. Small brass kettles for cooking have also become part of the equipment of most Cheyenne households.

By 1840, the Sioux and smallpox had almost totally annihilated both the Mandan and Hidatsa tribes. The Sioux had established themselves far west of the middle Missouri. With the disappearance of the Mandan villages as market centers, and the hazards interposed by the Sioux against reaching the Arikara villages, Cheyenne trading patterns are readjusting to new conditions. A string of American trading posts, or forts, have been established along the western stretches of the Platte River. They are more readily accessible to the Cheyennes, and somewhat to the south of the hostile Sioux. More importantly, the Hair Rope band, under the leadership of their band chief, Yellow Wolf, have crossed the Platte to the horse-rich country to the south. In 1828, Yellow Wolf showed the St. Louis–Santa Fe traders, William and Charles Bent and their partner Ceran St. Vrain, where to build a trading fort on the Arkansas River in southeastern Colorado. The great fort was finished in 1832, and the Hair Rope people and others moved permanently into a region of the Arkansas less than two hundred miles from the Texas border. The northern and southern bands now stretch over several hundred miles along the eastern face of the Rockies. Fort Laramie, established on the North Platte River by the American Fur Company, rival to the Bents and St. Vrain, draws the northern bands of Cheyennes into its orbit. The southerners are closely tied to Bent's Fort for their own profit and convenience. Tribal unity is still strong, but insidious forces of division are at work.

9 / Warfare

The Cheyennes fight to gain new hunting grounds as well as to hold such place as they have won for themselves on the Great Plains. They also fight to avenge earlier defeats and the deaths of relatives and friends, and they fight to advance their standings in the tribe as warriors and successful takers of horses from enemy tribes. Like all the nomadic tribes on the Plains, they are relatively recent newcomers to the great buffalo area, and with the Crows, Arapahos, Utes, Comanches, Shoshones, Pawnee, Omahas, Dakotas, and others, jostle for far-ranging hunting grounds. Each tribe maintains peaceful alliances with some tribes and an unrelenting struggle with others. The friendly allies of the Cheyennes are the three Village tribes of the upper Missouri River (Mandan, Hidatsa, and Arikara), the Sioux (formerly enemies), the cognate Arapaho, and, as we have seen, since 1840, the Comanche and Kiowa. Their foremost and despised enemy is the Crow tribe on the west, and then the Pawnee to the southeast. The Shoshones and Utes are next. The Sac, Fox, Delaware, and other displaced Woodland tribes, who were driven into the eastern Plains by the whites from 1836 onwards, are all treated as intruding enemies. The Cheyennes do not come up against them often, but they suffered severe defeats in 1853 at the hands of a few Delawares allied to the Pawnee, and again in 1854 at the hands of a hundred Sac and Fox. These eastern tribes are well armed with the best long-range buffalo rifles, which they handle with consummate skill and devastating effect against the Cheyennes, whose tactics are not well suited to the new style of warfare.

Living as they do in an atmosphere of chronic warfare, the Cheyennes, like other Plains tribes, emphasize military virtue. There are at least a hundred different situations in the ritual life of the people that invite ceremonial coup counting by an outstanding warrior. Public glory is the ever-present reward of the man who fights bravely and well. Public ridicule and scornful songs sung by the women drive on the young men. In the words of Stands in Timber:

> My grandfather and others used to tell me that hearing the women sing that way made them ready to do anything. It was hard to go into a fight, and they were often afraid, but it was worse to turn back and face the women. It was one reason they didn't show being scared, but went right in; they were forced to (Stands in Timber and Liberty 1967: 63).

The fighting patterns of the Cheyennes are embellished with virtuosities that go far beyond the needs of victory. Display in bravery tends to become an end in itself. Prestige drives override the more limited military requirements for defeat of the enemy. The show-off tends to supersede the mere soldier.

75

A Cheyenne camp. From a photograph by William S. Soulé, 1867-74. (Courtesy the Smithsonian Institution, Bureau of American Ethnology)

Cheyenne warriors, 1935. Photograph by E. A. Hoebel.

War has been transformed into a great game in which scoring against the enemy often takes precedence over killing him.

The scoring is in the counting of coup—touching or striking an enemy with hand or weapons. Coups counted within an enemy encampment rank highest of all. By extension, any heroic deed in battle counts as a coup: saving a wounded comrade, being first to locate the enemy, having a horse shot out from under one, or charging a body of enemies alone while the rest of the Cheyennes watch to see the result. A man's rank as a warrior depends on two factors: his total "score" in coups and his ability to lead successful raids in which Cheyenne losses are low. Actual killing and scalping get their credit, too, but they do not rate as highly as the show-off deeds. Closely allied to war is horse stealing, because any raid for horses can provoke a battle.

Cheyenne war parties are of three kinds: private, fraternity, and tribal. Of these, the first is by far the most common. Any properly qualified Cheyenne can assemble a war party; he need only engage the interest of a few friends. Since most men are caught up in the drive for military prestige, this is not hard to do—especially among the young men who still have their reputations to make. The older men who have secured their reputations and have responsibilities as peace chiefs or medicine men are not ordinarily so eager for the warpath as are the youngsters. The war leaders are those who have proven their skill on the warpath but who are not yet old enough or lack the personal attributes to be tribal chiefs or medicine men. The war chiefs are the officers of the military societies, but one does not have to have achieved that degree of eminence to lead a private war party. One needs only to be good.

Cheyenne custom does not require a vision endorsement of an inclination to lead a war party, as is true of some tribes. Nonetheless, as is the case with every important activity among the Cheyennes, a beginner must be instructed by a medicine man and must secure a ritualized right to undertake the mission. Cheyenne boys normally join their first war party when only fourteen or fifteen years of age. They are solicitously watched over by the older men and are not expected actively to engage in fighting, but they get their taste of danger and accumulate experience early. By twenty they are seasoned warriors. By thirty, or earlier, they are ready to lead their own raids, if they have the necessary leadership qualities.

When the time comes, an aspiring war leader invites an experienced older man to help him. He offers his pipe and explains his wish. Most commonly he is told to make an offering to the Sacred Arrows, or perhaps to hang himself from a pole in the hills. If it is to be an offering to the Arrows, he fills his pipe, dons a buffalo robe hair side out, and walks to the lodge of the Arrow Keeper, wailing as he goes, so that everyone will know what he is about. At the door of the lodge, he stands and wails until the Arrow Keeper invites him in. The Keeper smokes the suppliant's pipe, thereby acknowledging his readiness to help him. The suppliant ritually consecrates the offering, which, under the Keeper's direction, is then tied to the Arrow Bundle. During the course of this act, the young man prays to the Arrows, asking for success in his new venture.

Now he is ready to lead war parties. He calls together some friends and other men who he thinks will make good and willing companions. First, he feeds them. Then he tells them what is in his mind. He passes his pipe, and all who have decided to accept his leadership smoke. The others pass it by.

After a while, those who have pledged themselves go together to the tipi of a ceremonial priest or some good medicine man for ritual preparation. They take him a filled pipe, telling him they wish to go to war. If he approves the plan, he smokes and sings a sacred war song. He may tell them which way to go and where they may expect to find their enemies. They now have "official" sanction for their venture.

Still later, they may bring some war article—a shield, bonnet, or weapon— to be consecrated in a sweat lodge as a talisman of good luck and protection. Various members of the party may cut strips of skin from their arms to leave as sacrifices to the spiritual powers.

Now they get ready their gear. The night before their departure, painted and stripped for action, they parade around the camp, singing wolf songs—for the wolf is associated with war—and receiving little presents from the people who wish them well.

A war party of this type is breaking itself off from the society for a while. Consequently, it does not leave as a body, nor is there any display at the time of the departure. The leader starts out alone early the next day. The members have an appointed rendezvous not far from the first night's camping place. From this spot, they all proceed together in single file, with the leader in front carrying his pipe. At the camp site they smoke, pray, and sing holy war songs. At last, when all the others are asleep, the leader chants a prayer for help, courage, and wisdom.

So they proceed until they reach the danger ground. Once there, they move by cautious stages, with two scouts well in advance. These move under cover to an elevation where they can scrutinize the country ahead. They not only look for human beings, camps, and smoke, but they study the actions of birds and animals for the characteristic signs and actions they show when people are near. If all is clear, the scouts signal their followers to advance, while they move on to the next point of observation.

Small, private raiding parties of this kind are out either to take horses or to get a scalp in revenge for the death of a friend or relative. If the first object is their goal, they seek to avoid a fight and will sneak into the enemy camp at night to drive off its herd under the cover of darkness. If it is scalps they are after, they prefer to come upon lone travelers, small isolated family camps, or parties of hunters. If they find a camp, and they are not discovered, they take time to prepare their war medicines and paint themselves. Otherwise, they attack as the opportunity offers.

Big war parties are almost always revenge expeditions. When a Cheyenne raiding party has been wiped out or a considerable number of casualties have been suffered by an attack on a Cheyenne camp, someone is almost sure to get a hundred or more warriors together for a punitive expedition. He takes his pipe from camp to camp, gathering recruits. Or he may go to several military societies to enlist their members. Such an outfit is still essentially a private war party, because it is the affair of the man who initiates it.

Because the membership of the military societies is (with the exception of the Dog Soldiers) scattered through all the bands, war parties are rarely con- stituted of members from one fraternity only. It may be also that the disas- trous annihilation of the Bowstring Soldiers by the Kiowas in 1837 discouraged what might have been a more prevalent practice in earlier times. In the Cheyenne's mind, that event proves the power of the Sacred Arrows and the disastrous effects of disrespect for them. The Cheyennes and Arapahos were camped together near Bents' Fort while the Arapahos were holding a Sun Dance. No Cheyenne war parties had been out for some time, because there had been a killing in the tribe. An Arrow Renewal had been pledged, but Grey Thunder, the Arrow Keeper, was postponing the rite until the Arapaho ceremony was finished. Restless Cheyenne warriors were not interested in the Arapaho doings; they wanted their Arrows renewed so that they could get off to war. The Bowstrings were especially eager. At last the Bowstrings arrogantly demanded that the Arrows be renewed, and when Grey Thunder refused, they actually beat him. He then consented, but prophesied disaster for them. The war party of forty-two Bowstrings, after a long and exhausting trip on foot during which they used up most of their arrows hunting game, finally found a big Kiowa camp. Their scouts were seen before they were ready to attack, and the Kiowas greatly outnumbered them. As a result, the Cheyennes were cut off and forced to make a stand. With few arrows they could not long defend themselves, and so died to a man.

This is the kind of loss that provokes the entire tribe to go on the warpath in revenge. In this particular case, Porcupine Bear, head chief of the Dog Soldiers, undertook to organize the war party. He set out to devote the winter to the task, carrying his pipe and a barrel of whiskey obtained from some trader. The whiskey was his undoing, for at one camp there was a drunken brawl and Porcupine Bear and six of his relatives killed a man. He was exiled, and his close kin went with him. After the Renewal of the Arrows in the summer of 1838, Little Wolf, chief of the Bowstrings (later the Sweet Medicine Chief of the entire tribe), took up the task. So much time was required to call in the northern bands that by the time they were assembled, winter was again at hand. The camp circle was at last complete, and a large arbor for the military societies was placed in its center. Here all the fraternities convened to receive the relatives of the forty-two dead men, who came to them with horses and presents. Their arms streaming blood from their mourning gashes (see page 93), the women passed their reeking hands over the soldiers, asking them to take pity on them. The soldiers agreed. But then came a big snow, and the tribe had to break up, for there was not feed enough for all the horses. When spring came, they reassembled.

On a tribal war move, the Arrow and Buffalo Hat Bundles play an important part. They are carried on the backs of their Keepers' wives, and four stops must be made for their ritual use. Before the big attack, after the enemy has been sighted, there is a massive ritual preparation of the Arrows culminating in the pointing of the two man Arrows at the enemy, who, it will be remembered, are supposed to be blinded by their brightness and confused by their power. The Arrows are then lashed to the lance of a great warrior and carried by him into the thick of the battle. The Buffalo Hat is worn by another warrior—and so success is assured, although in fact it does not always work out that way.

It is often said that Indians fight as a howling, unorganized mob, each man for himself. This is not true in general, and certainly not true for the Cheyennes in particular. The tactics of attack and battle are carefully planned by the leaders, and when faithfully carried out often result in a successful clash. The Cheyennes do not ordinarily aim for total victory, but for glory, revenge, and the inflicting of some humiliation and punishment on the enemy. Set battles are therefore avoided, and the tactics are those of stealth, surprise, and maneuver. If the enemy is alerted and well prepared behind earthworks or in a camp with the tipis set edge to edge as a defensive fortification, the Cheyennes will not ordinarily come to close grips with them. Since the aims of their war do not call for "taking" an enemy position, they withdraw to try again another time. The tribal numbers are small and they cannot stand too many battle losses. Yet, many do vow to die in battle—the suicide vow. In the great attack on the Crows in 1820, Two Twists, who had organized the affair, had vowed to drive the Crows out of their breastworks and die doing it. While all the Cheyennes watched, he charged alone straight into the Crow camp, armed only with a sabre. He fought like a demon and could not be brought down (largely because it happened that most of the Crow fighters were away on their own warpath). Fired by his example, the other Cheyennes charged and broke through, killing or capturing everyone in the camp.

Many unforeseen events may upset the plans of the Cheyenne war leaders, but the most plaguing difficulty is the propensity of the scouts to attack enemy stragglers in an effort to get a coup. Too often the result is that the enemy is alerted and the planned strategy upset. The leader of a private war party can do nothing about this. On the tribal moves, however, the enterprise is policed; scouts who slip in such a way are beaten just as though they had broken the rules of the communal hunt.

Cheyenne feats of bravery are legendary. Yet the Cheyennes are by no means supermen. They live from day to day knowing that every hunt exposes them to unannounced attack; every night when they lie down to rest they know that dawn will bring the possibility of an enemy attack on their herds or on their camp. For them, there is no such thing as security—ever. There are no interludes of peace to give surcease from war. When the lurking threat of enemy attacks is not working on them, there is always the knowledge that to qualify as men at all they must themselves go seek out the enemy. Fear haunts them, even though they rarely let it break through to the surface. The evidence is everywhere—the masochistic tortures of hanging from the pole to bring good luck in war, the offering up of cut strips from the arms before starting on the warpath, the faith in the blinding powers of the Arrows, the elaborate rules of smoking and painting in connection with the warpath, the reliance on amulets and tabus to give immunity in battle, the great store set by medicine shields. Grinnell thinks the shield is perhaps the most important part of the equipment of the Cheyenne warrior:

> Most shields were believed to possess strong spiritual power. It might exercise in behalf of him who carried it not only the general protective influence due to its sacred character, but it might also endue him with those qualities attributed to the heavenly bodies, birds, mammals, and other living creatures whose images were painted on it, or portions of which were tied to it. . . . A shield adorned with the feathers of the eagle was believed to give its owner the swiftness and courage of that bird. If the feathers of the owl were tied on it, the man perhaps shared the owl's power to see in the dark, and to move silently and unnoticed. The figure of a bear painted on the shield, or its claws attached, gave him the bear's toughness; and so many of the qualities which belonged to the animals which the Cheyennes regarded as possessing superhuman powers (Grinnell 1923:I, 187–188).

Cheyenne shields are of two major classes: the sacred shields, just described, and ordinary, undecorated shields which are without power. The first class also subdivides into traditional shields belonging to a warrior society or kindred. The group shields of a particular organization are all similar. The second subcategory consists of dream shields, the pattern and power of which have been revealed to their owners in visions.

The technical construction of all shields is alike. The hide of a buffalo bull is thickened and toughened by steaming. The finished shield is round and only eighteen inches or so in diameter. If it is a power shield, it requires an antelope-hide cover on which the medicine symbols are painted.

No man may decorate a shield for the first time without the aid and direction of an established shield maker, who has himself acquired the right by previous instruction. The actual shield painting requires ritual help and dedication by a number of other brave fighters. They decorate themselves with bird feathers and shut themselves in the shield maker's lodge with him. The process begins with ceremonial smoking and the singing of a sacred song. The shield owner then paints a part of his design, after which the pipe is refilled and everyone smokes around the circle. Four songs are sung, and the painting is resumed. This cycle is repeated again and again, until the painting is finished. At last, the cover is fitted to the shield, and the feathers and other objects are added. When this has been done, everyone rubs himself all over with white clay in a first step toward removing the supernatural atmosphere so that he may again enter into ordinary affairs. The female relatives of the owner pass in food, and they eat.

The shield is now put near the door of the lodge where it may be touched by a multitude of men, women, and children, who are called in to get a share of its protective effect. The ceremony is completed with a final purification in which the shield is placed on top of a sweat lodge, raised a few yards in front of the tipi, and all the participants in the painting take a sweat bath while singing sacred shield songs.

A shield thereafter receives very special treatment. It is not kept in its owner's lodge, but rests on a tripod or pole outside of it. Each shield has its special requirements of preparation for use. The owner of one shield told a borrower that it had to be purified in juniper smoke before using. In addition,

> When you put the cover on, the deerskin strings which hold the bearclaws must be loosened, so that they may lie down; but when you take the cover off, and go into a fight, the strings must be tightened, so that the claws will stand out stiff, and be directed toward the enemy. When purifying the shield you must pass it over the smoke in the four directions and last hold it over the smoke, and then raise it toward the sky and shake it. Then you must move it four times toward the right front of your body, and hang it over your body on the right side. In riding forward toward the enemy, you must keep on the right-hand side of your party, and quite away from them. Some shields may be supported on a single pole, but this must be on a tripod. In the morning it must be hung out facing the sun (Grinnell 1923:I, 194).

This is but one reason why the Cheyennes need time to prepare their powers before going into battle. Failure to fulfill any one requirement will almost certainly cause a man to be wounded or killed. The misuse of a shield requires a long, and sometimes strong, ceremony of atonement and purification. The group shields of the Hair Rope band impose an injunction against eating the heart of any animal, or any meat that has been boiled in a stew along with heart. If the prohibition is violated, the shield user must eat the heart of an enemy—something the Cheyenne finds difficult and disagreeable to do.

The Cheyennes did not originally have war bonnets, but began to adopt them towards the end of the climax period. War bonnets have essentially the same quality as shields; they are not just something that is made and worn. The great Dog Soldier chief, Roman Nose, owed something of his success to his war bonnet, which gave him immunity to bullets. With this bonnet went the tabu that he could eat no food taken from the pot with a pointed, iron utensil. The psychological association is clear. As the pointed implement pierces the food, so will a pointed metal bullet pierce the flesh. Just before the big fight with Colonel Forsythe's command at Beecher Island in 1868, Roman Nose had been entertained in the Sioux camp. Ignorant of his guest's tabus, his host served him fried bread taken from the pan with a fork. A Dog Soldier noticed it and told Roman Nose. The fight with the Americans began before Roman Nose was able to go through his long purificatory rite, so, like Achilles, he stayed in his tent while the battle dragged on. Finally, he gave in to the pleas that he come forth to lead his men. He put on his war bonnet, and while riding up to the battlefield, he was shot and mortally wounded. He did not even get into the fight (Grinnell 1915:275–277).

War ponies must also be supernaturally fortified, if they are to be of the best quality. A man who is well equipped with a string of horses rarely rides his favorite battle steed except in a fight. When off on a mounted raid, he rides an ordinary horse and leads his fighting pony. To insure the quality of such a horse, he selects a yearling that has good prospects and takes it with his pipe to a shaman who has horse medicine. He tells the medicine man he has vowed not to ride the horse for several months, and asks to have it dedicated. After smoking, the medicine man tells him something like this:

> Every night, lead him in and groom him well. Then just turn him loose. He'll run right back to the herd. When he runs back, you get on a hill and watch him. If he lies down, rolls around, and gets up and shakes himself, he is showing that he knows you have promised him something. If you really mean what you have promised here, go out and kill a buck antelope. Take one prong of the horns. We will polish it down and bore a hole in it. Then I will get *mutstintants* to fill the horn with. Fasten two buckskin thongs to the horn and tie it snugly about your pony's neck. If it gets tight, loosen it; it shows that your pony is fattening. Do not ride him at all until the time is up. Then bring him to me (Hoebel n.d.).

When the promised time has elapsed, the owner leads the horse to the medicine man. He talks to the pony, saying, "Now your months are up. He is going to ride you. Wherever he goes, he'll take you with him." To dedicate a horse and then break the promise not to ride it before its time will kill the horse and bring its owner bad luck.

This performance reveals clearly the Cheyenne feeling about male sexuality—that it is something to be husbanded and kept in reserve as a source of strength for the great crises of war. *Mutstintants* is a root of the species *Cogswellia,* the Cheyenne name of which refers to *motse,* the term for a male, or breeder, among large animals; in other words, the Cheyennes associate this root with animal virility and strength. The phallic symbolism of the antelope horn and the powdered root within it is anything but obscure.

The Scalp Dance that follows a successful raid by a large war party shows in turn how the Cheyennes associate victory with sex properly controlled. Scalping among American Indians is the equivalent of head hunting in other parts of the world. The purpose of both head taking and scalping is to add the supernatural power and life force of the victim to that of the victor.

The Cheyenne Scalp Dance is run by the tribal berdaches, or transvestites, as masters of ceremony. The transvestites are males who wear women's clothes and often serve as second wives in a married man's household. The Cheyennes call them *hemaneh*, Halfman-halfwoman. There are only five of these in the tribe, all members of the same kindred, the Bare Legs family. They are all doctors and highly respected. War parties like to have Halfmen-halfwomen along, not only for their medical skill, but because they are socially graceful and entertaining. Young people like them because they possess the most powerful of all love medicines. A suitor who is able to get their help is fortunate indeed, for no girl can resist the power of their potions. They are especially sought out as intermediaries to lead the gift-laden horses to a girl's household when a marriage proposal is being made. These people, through sexual sublimation—with their abstinence and denial of their original sex—seem to achieve great power. Although we have no *direct* evidence for it, it appears probable that their presence on war parties is desired mainly because of their high "psychological" potential of stored-up virility—which is just what the Cheyennes feel is necessary for successful fighting.

A successful war party is one which has taken enemy scalps without the loss of a single Cheyenne, unless the dead Cheyenne had counted coup before being killed. If but one Cheyenne is killed without first counting coup, any scalps the others have taken are thrown away. If, however, the Cheyennes have been successful in the fighting, with scalps and no losses, the scalps are brought back for a Scalp Dance. The fact that on the return from the battle all the scalps are placed in the custody of the Halfmen-halfwomen indicates that the warriors feel their success is due to the presence of these personages. The fact that the victory dance is a courting dance wholly directed by the Halfmen-halfwomen emphasizes the relation of war to virility. The affirmation of power over their enemies is the assertion of Cheyenne virility. It is for this that virility must be husbanded and receives its apotheosis in the victory celebration of the Dance of the Scalps.

The Scalp Dance is no wild, frenzied affair (as most outsiders imagine it to be); rather, it is a sociable courtship dance, made up of several parts. It takes place about a huge bonfire prepared by the transvestites, and called a "skunk." The singers for the dance are middle-aged men, all married. They stand in a line to the west of the skunk, facing east. The young men line up north of the fire, the young girls across from them, on the south. Old men and women fill in the eastern side of the square. Only the Halfmen-halfwomen, with their scalps on scalp poles in their hands, are allowed within the square.

The first dance is the Sweetheart's Dance. The young men file around the drummers and line up behind the girls. Each takes the arm of a girl partner, and they dance side by side. The old men and women dance by themselves in their places, some of the women dancing with scalps taken in previous raids. The Halfmen-halfwomen dance before the drummers, waving the newly won scalps. The old men and women clown and burlesque their dancing, trying to make the watchers laugh.

The Courtship, or Sweetheart Dance, is followed by a Matchmaking Dance. In this dance, the old people only look on. The Halfmen-halfwomen split up and go down the lines of boys and girls, asking them who their favorite partners might be. They compare notes in the center, while the dancers wait expectantly. Now they go to the boys, and one by one lead them by their robes to stand next to the girls who are designated for them. Girls and boys are alternated in the line. When every girl has a partner, the dancing begins. Here the girls dance alone, with their backs to the boys. They first dance forward, to the center of the square, and then backward, without turning, to their places beside the boys. There is nothing intimate about this, nothing remotely sensual; it is as formal as the Cheyenne marriage bid. The boys may attain proximity to the girls, but the girls dance away from them, back and away, back and away. Courting is an uncertain business.

A Round Dance is next. On command of the transvestites, the two lines of boys and girls dance up to each other, and then away, but still facing each other. The girls are not so coy or quite so elusive. This movement goes on for some time, when the "callers" cry out, "Choose your partners." Each girl and boy moves across the square to the one for whom he or she had been chosen in the Match-making Dance. Now they all form a circle with their arms about each others' waists. With short, side-stepping movements they dance clockwise, with the old folks in the middle, whooping and hollering, and waving their scalps. The transvestites keep back the children, who crowd too close to watch, by waving their scalps at them from outside the circle.

After a while, the pattern is changed. The Halfmen-halfwomen call, "Girls to the middle and the men to close up." The boys have "captured" their mates. They dance in a ring around the girls while every once in a while the bolder ones among them slip into the middle and hug their girls, arms around their necks. When there has been enough of this, they break up, and all parties go back to form the beginning square.

Now follows what the Cheyennes call the Slippery Dance. It, too, is replete with symbolic significance. Mating is a reciprocal affair. In the previous dance, the boys showed they had the girls. Now the girls show they have got their men. Dancing in pairs, the girls move up to the line of boys, each getting a good hold on the robe of her partner and leading him out to the center. As the girls dance, the young men tag meekly along in tow. They stay that way until their sisters come out to "set them free" by making a present of a bracelet or ring to the girls who have their brothers. Thus, female siblings assert their claim on their brothers, but at a price paid to his new "wife." Wives' rights to a man's loyalty take precedence over his sister's, but a sister is not cut off entirely by his marriage.

The final dance, signifying the culmination of courtship and mating, is the Galloping Buffalo Bull Dance. The women take time out to tie their long skirts up around their legs; then the leaders tell everyone to sit down in his place. The drumming and singing begin. Three or four women get up and go over to where the young men are sitting. They bend over, turn around, and dance with their backs to the men, dancing like buffalo. Soon the men—as many as there are women dancing—spring up, and stooping over like buffalo bulls go prancing along behind the women. More and more women lead on the men, until all the dancers are bounding in a long row like a worked-up

herd of buffalo. At last, the Halfmen-halfwomen call, "Go 'round in a circle."
Everybody stands up and goes into the Round Dance, and drummers and
singers, mating couples and old people, are reunited in one, closed, happy,
collective unity. They all sing together as they dance and morning dawns.

D. World View and Cheyenne Personality

10 / World view and religion

The major orientations of the Cheyenne world view and some of its manifestations in religious and ritual behavior have already been revealed in earlier chapters. In this chapter and the following, we shall more explicitly examine the underlying assumptions formulated by the Cheyennes as to the nature of the universe and man.

Gregory Bateson has rightly written, "The human individual is endlessly simplifying and generalizing his own view of his environment; *he constantly imposes on this environment his own constructions and meanings;* these constructions and meanings are characteristic of one culture as opposed to another" (quoted in Kluckhohn 1949:356, italics ours). Or, as Kluckhohn has phrased it,

> Each different way of life makes its own assumptions about the ends and purposes of human existence, about ways by which knowledge may be obtained, about the organization of the pigeonholes in which each sense datum is filed, about what human beings have a right to expect from each other and the gods, about what constitutes fulfillment or frustration. Some of these assumptions are made explicit in the lore of the folk; others are tacit premises which the observer must infer by finding consistent trends in word and deed (Kluckhohn 1949:359).

Such assumptions and premises are the basic postulates underlying each culture: postulates which define the nature of things are classed as existential postulates; those which qualitatively fix the desirability or undesirability of things or acts are normative postulates. Human perception and human evaluation are colored and shaped by the underlying cultural postulates which are the foundation of knowledge and belief. Human beings see all things through culturally tinted lenses.

In examining the major Cheyenne assumptions and values, we find first a rather striking combination of vitalistic and mechanistic attitudes toward the universe.

The Cheyenne world of experience is a dynamic, operative system of interrelated parts. Altogether, these parts form the universe, which the Cheyennes call *hestenov*. The universe is multilayered. Human beings view the universe from the Earth's surface. All above the Earth's surface is *heammahestonev*. All that lies below it is *aktunov*. Along the surface of the earth is a thin layer of air, the atmosphere as perceived by the Cheyennes. Called *taxtavo*, it is a special gift of the spirit beings to humankind, for it makes breathing and life possible. Above the air-layer is *setovo*, the Nearer Sky Space. It is more or less equivalent to the earth's physical atmosphere as known to modern science. It is here that one finds the clouds, the winds, the birds, and the holy places

87

atop high hills and mountains. Above everything else is the Blue Sky Space, *aktovo*. Here are visible the sun, the moon, the stars, and the Milky Way.

The earth itself consists of two layers. The first is the very thin strip which supports life. It is only as deep as the roots of plants and trees can penetrate. It is known as *votoso*. Beneath it is the stratum called *aktunov*, the Deep Earth.

From the religious point of view, each level is suffused with spirit forces, or is the home of spirit beings which are mystic counterparts to various physical phenomena which are characteristic of the level in question.

In the Blue Sky Space, for example, there is the sun. The Cheyenne call it *esehe*, Day Sun. It is born in the east every morning and may be seen by anyone. The visible sun is the concrete manifestation of the Sun Spirit (or God), who is called *Atovsz*. The sun, therefore, is both a thing and a spirit being, each of which has a distinctive name. *Atovsz*, who is very powerful, can appear to some human beings by taking the form of a man. The moon is known as *taesehe*, or Night Sun. It is born in the west every twenty-eight nights. It, too, can be seen by everyone. The visible moon, like the sun, has its spirit being, *Ameonito*, the Moon Spirit (or God). It, too, can make an appearance in the form of a human being, if it wishes to favor some person.

Certain planets, such as the Morning Star and Evening Star, are especially revered. In the case of the Morning and Evening Stars, it is because of their close associations with the Sun and Moon Spirits. Various constellations figure in myths and ceremonies for their parts in the lives of the ancient Cheyennes and their roles in lives of the living.

The Milky Way is a conspicuous feature of cloudless night skies—especially above the open plains. To the Cheyennes, it is *ekutsihimmiyo*, the Hanging Road, suspended between the Blue Sky Space and Earth. It is the road along which the souls of the dead travel to the afterlife.

However many spirit beings there may be in the several strata of the air and sky parts of the universe—those which together make up *heammahestov*—they are but particular expressions of the great, all-pervading, all-knowing High God, *Heammawihio,* The Wise One Above. *Wihio* means spider. "The spider spins a web, and goes up and down, seemingly walking on nothing" (Grinnell 1923:II,89). *Wihio* as a stem "appears to embody the idea of mental ability of an order higher than common-superior intelligence." *Heammawihio* is the supreme deity, because he knows more about how to do things than do all other creatures. Long ago, he left the earth and retired to the sky. The sun is believed to represent *Heammawihio*, although the deity is a good deal more than the sun; he is an abstraction, not just a super-brilliant, heat-radiating celestial sphere. The first offering of the pipe is made to him in all smoking.

Beneath the surface of the Earth, the Deep Earth, *aktuno*, has its own spirituality. It is female in principle and is governed by *Heammawihio's* Deep Earth counterpart, *Aktunowihio.*

When the Cheyennes think of the universe along the horizontal plane, they divide it into the four cardinal directions: south, east, north, and west. The south and east are associated with warmth (red), with light, and with green, growing things. The north is associated with cold and the white of winter. The west is ominous with the blue-black of death and night. Each of these areas has its own particular spirits (see pp. 49–50).

The color symbolism of the major directions and their seasonal changes is far too complex and esoteric for us to try to describe or explain it here. It is said that only the Cheyenne priests understand it fully.

An important feature of Cheyenne religious belief is that any one of the major (and also the minor) spirits, although they are usually manifest as natural phenomena (sun, moon, and so on) can also appear in the form of a human being—frequently as an old man or woman, or as a handsome youth or beautiful young maiden.

Birds are apt to have sacred powers and are revered because they live in the Nearer Sky Space. Animals have lesser powers, except for burrowing animals, such as the badger who penetrates the Deep Earth, and the bear who lives in caves. The holiness of the buffalo derives from the Cheyenne belief that they originated in a great underground cave (a notion borrowed from the Mandan). Indeed, it should be remembered that Sweet Medicine was taught the forms of Cheyenne culture by *Maiyun* during his long sojourn in the cave in Bear Butte.

The major view of the Cheyenne universe is thus animistic—a belief in spirit beings. All the spirits together are commonly spoken of as though they constitute a single supernatural entity, *Maiyun*, although they also exist and can operate separately. The great objective of religious practice is to relate to the spirit beings in such ways that life will be enhanced. It is assumed by the Cheyennes that most spirit beings are beneficent; they want things to be pleasant and satisfying. They are generous in their blessings upon mankind. They are not niggardly and withholding by nature. They are not vindictive, punishing, cruel, or fearsome; although there are things to be feared, neither Cheyenne religion nor world view rests on fear of the "Gods." Nor are they creators. Cheyenne mythology gives scant attention to questions of how the world was made. It *is*. The great attributes of the spirits lie, rather, in their *knowledge*. They know how to make the universe run properly and how to get the most out of it. Their role, therefore, is that of instructor of men. They are the great teachers. This concept expresses the Cheyenne view that the universe is essentially a mechanical system which is good in essence, but which must be properly understood and used to keep it producing what humans need and want. The great spirits understand the nature of its working; they know the techniques that help it to produce. This knowledge they willingly share with mankind, if mankind seeks and listens respectfully. Thus the culture-hero myths centering on Sweet Medicine and Erect Horns are accounts of pilgrimages to the fountainheads of knowledge, the homes of the Holy Ones in the Sacred Mountain. The point is important: the greatness of the major spirits is not in their ability supernaturally to create and manage things, but in their wisdom about the working of things.

So it is that the great rituals were taught to the legendary knowledge seekers, who in turn carefully taught them to their fellow Cheyennes. So it is that one who has learned a ritual becomes a teacher in the later performances of that ritual. The Pledger of an Arrow Renewal or a Sun Dance, the Quiller of a first robe, is taught step by step the performance of the rite. Even the leader of a first war party must learn the preliminary rites from a knowledgeable priest. Every Cheyenne ritual of consequence has at least a Teacher and a Novice in its personnel.

In content, Cheyenne rituals are compulsive actions rather than verbal petitions. As stated by the Reverend Rudolph Petter, a Mennonite missionary with an intimate knowledge of the Cheyennes based upon many years of association with them, "In religious ceremonies, the rites, not the words, are of most importance" (Petter 1907:477). The acts are effective forces in themselves; they work directly upon the mechanical system of the universe. As an analogy, we might say that the Cheyenne ceremonies are "tune-up jobs," or—in the case of the Arrow Renewal Rites—major overhauls of a machine that has got out of adjustment or suffered a major breakdown in one of its parts.

There is no evidence that the Cheyennes have any explicit energy theory, but it is clearly evident that they have some sort of an implicit energy concept. The total energy charge of any object, and of the world itself, is thought of as limited. As it is expended through activity, it is dissipated and diminished. Thus plants wither, animals become scarce, the earth runs down. Renewal through regeneration is necessary, if the people are to survive. The ceremonies produce a recharge and readjustment of the parts so that the whole operates at its full potential once more.

This notion is clearly revealed in the Cheyenne attitude toward sex. Sexual energy is a limited quotient which must be spent sparingly. Therefore, the man of strong character and good family vows at the birth of his first child (especially if it is a boy) not to have another child for either seven or fourteen years. All of the father's growth powers are then concentrated on the development of this one child rather than being dissipated among several. It is necessary to understand that more than the semen of conception goes into growing a child; there is continuing transfer of the father's "energy" from parent to offspring. The dedication of a child by this means is quite similar to the development of the war pony (described in the last chapter) through abstention and ritual performance. During the long period of seven or fourteen years the father must practice absolute celibacy, unless he has more than one wife. The mother of the dedicated child is without question celibate throughout the period, unless her husband pledges an Arrow Renewal or Sun Dance, when for that specific occasion she may engage in sexual union with the instructing priest. Adultery is so rare among the Cheyennes that it hardly provides an available, if irregular, outlet for sexual desires. Should a parent break the vow of dedication, it is believed it will kill the child. Not many Cheyenne men feel strong enough to submit themselves to the test of self-control demanded for the sake of a child in this act of renunciation, but for those who do, there is the highest of social esteem. My own close friend, High Forehead, was one who did it. There was, in fact, a fifteen-year gap between the birth of his first and second child. His eldest son, when I knew him, was a most superior individual, physically and mentally. High Forehead was quietly proud of the part he felt he played in making him so. "I slept with my wife all that time," he told me, "but I never had sexual relations with her." In his old age, he was one of the most honored men among the Northern Cheyennes.

The Cheyenne in no sense believes that he can control nature. Although the environment is hard and life is precarious, it is looked upon as a good environment. It is one, however, with which people must keep in close tune through careful and tight self-control. Sweet Medicine and Erect Horns warned the ancients of the decline of the Cheyennes which would take place if they failed to act as they were instructed. The prescribed motions and symbolic acts of the numerous ceremonies must be exactly performed as set in tradition, if they are to produce the desired results in earth regeneration, good health, good hunts, and victory. "If the sacred acts were not performed correctly and in proper order . . . it was the obligation of the members of the ceremony to intervene.

If all of the officiants erred, a strong wind would arise to warn them of a breach" (Anderson 1956:98). Here, then, is a behavioral response to the Cheyenne view of the mechanics of their systematic universe. Human aspirations are realizable not so much through the appeasement of whimsical spirit beings and gods as through action that fits the conditions of environmental organization and functioning. Man must fit his behavior to the requirements of those conditions, which are impersonal, rather than seek an emotional dependence upon individual creatures. In this respect, the Cheyenne view of the universe has much in common with that of the Pueblo Indians, except that Puebloans feel much more strongly that individual misbehavior throws the whole universe out of balance. The Cheyennes apply this latter notion only to intratribal killings.

The Cheyenne medicine man is consequently more of a priest than he is a shaman. The main road to supernatural power is through acquisition of ritual knowledge learned from one who is already a priest. Such knowledge is technical knowledge, effective when put to use as a "manual of procedures."

Nonetheless, a component of vitalistic animism is also present in the Cheyenne world view. Individual Cheyennes do seek supernatural power on the vision quest; they do share the Guardian Spirit Complex so characteristic of many other North American tribes. A man who wants personal power for healing or immunity in battle may fast in a lonely place and beg the spirits for indulgence and aid. If favored by a spirit, he receives a blessing along with instructions as to how to prepare specific amulets and how to paint himself and what to sing to evoke the power. He is further given the tabus that qualify its use and protection. Visions also come unsought in time of distress, as in the case of the girl who founded the tribal council, or the case of Owl Friend, who founded a new Bowstring Soldier Society on the basis of a dream that came upon him as he lay exhausted in the snow when lost in a blizzard. Guardian spirits are called *maiyunahu'ta*, Spirit Who Told Me in Sleep. The individual Cheyenne who wishes to become in tune with the animistic powers of the universe, however, does it not so much through fasting and vision seeking as through the sacrificial offering. The pledging of a ceremony is an offering in exchange for help. Gifts are given to the Medicine Arrows and Sun Dance Lodge. Skin is cut from the arms, and men hang from the pole or drag buffalo skulls.

> One offered to the *maiyu*[n] . . . food, tobacco, a blanket or some calico, or a white bison hide, an arrow or a root digger, an enemy scalp, a finger joint, a strip or [*sic*] skin or a bit of flesh, or a ritual or ceremony. . . . In a narrow sense it was giving; *in a wider sense, simply doing, that which was valued by the supernaturals.* The gifts or acts were traditional and standard, which is to say, culturally prescribed; *the goal or response was a concrete return*—health for oneself or kin, a wealth of horses, many coups on a raid, success in the hunt, or a shaman's powers (Anderson 1956:102; italics ours).

The important point is that even the Cheyenne spirit beings respond to acts in a quite mechanical way.

Although of lesser importance, we should mention that the Earth Surface layer contains some nuisance spirits. These are the *minio,* Horned Hairy Water Spirits, and ghosts. The *minio* sometimes seize people in rivers and lakes, but in some stories at least, the Thunderbird, swiftly diving from the sky, sets them free. The *minio* are bogey-like creatures; they really do not figure greatly in Cheyenne affairs, but the idea of possible contact with them frightens the more credulous Cheyennes.

Ghosts make the Cheyenne uneasy. Ghosts, or *mistai*, are spirits derived from the dead, but they are not the ghosts of particular people. The *mistai* are really poltergeists. They make their presence known by whistling and making weird noises; in the very dark places, especially in the woods, they tug at one's robe; they tap and scratch on lodge coverings. In other words, they are the night noises and sensations that make even the most skeptical of us a bit jumpy when alone in the house at night or walking down a solitary dark street or lane.

The soul of a person is far different. It is his *tasoom*, his shadow or shade, the vital substance and spiritual essence of the body. When it leaves the body for any length of time, death comes. Death is not personified as a being. It is simply the state of existence after the *tasoom* has separated from the body. The *tasoom* travels to the home of *Heammawihio* by way of *ekutsihimmiyo*, The Hanging Road. All the Cheyennes of the past live in heaven, just as they did on earth—and have a good time of it. As happens among many other American Indians, occasional Cheyennes who are close to death fall into a coma during which they later believe themselves to have visited the villages of those who are really dead. They are "sent back to earth" by the spirit people, and recover with vivid impressions of their experience.

For the Cheyenne there is no Hell or punishment of any sort in afterlife; no Judgment or Damnation. Although Cheyennes sin when they commit murder and they often do wrong, murder is expiated in the here and now, and wrong-doing builds up no burden of guilt to be borne beyond the grave. For the Cheyenne there is no problem of salvation; goodness is to be sought as rightness for its own sake and for the appreciative approval of one's fellow man. When at last it is free of its corporal abode, the Cheyenne soul wafts free and light up the Hanging Road to dwell thereafter in benign proximity to the Great Wise One and the long-lost loved ones. Only the souls of those who have committed suicide are barred from this peace. When these souls reach the fork in the Milky Way, their course is diverted along the branch which leads not to Heaven but to nothingness. Of course, warriors who have taken the suicide vow to die in battle do not suffer this fate.

In spite of the happy destination that awaits the dead, death is clearly a traumatic experience for the surviving relatives. Each individual is highly valued, for the population is small, and every loss is keenly felt. This is why revenge drives are so strong against enemies who kill Cheyennes.

The corpse of one who had died in camp is quickly disposed of, for people feel that its spirit will not start its journey to the Milky Way until the body has been removed to its final resting place. In other words, the spirit does not take leave of the tribe until the final act of physical separation is complete. It is believed, further, that spirits like company on their journey and that some of them try to take the spirit of a living person with them, and, hence, if the body is not disposed of with alacrity, someone may die. Children are especially susceptible to this danger.

Cheyenne burials are bundle burials. Relatives and close friends dress the body of the deceased in its finest clothing. They wrap it, extended full length with the arms at the sides, in a number of robes lashed round about with great lengths of ropes. The burial bundle is transported by travois (a vehicle made of two trailing poles supporting a platform) to its place of deposit some distance from the camp. It may be placed either in the crotch of a tree or upon a scaffold. Or it may be covered over with rocks on the ground. The owner's favorite horses are shot and left at the grave along with his weapons, or, in the case of a woman, her utensils. A man's shield and war bonnet are usually left to his son or best friend; a woman's flesher is left to her daughter. Everything else is given away, usually to nonrelatives who come to the survivor's lodge to mourn until everything has been disposed of, including the lodge. (See Llewellyn and Hoebel 1941:212–213 for the details of Cheyenne inheritance practices.)

The mourning customs fall most heavily on the women. Female relatives, especially mothers and wives, cut off their long hair and gash their foreheads so that the blood flows. If the dead one had been killed by enemies, they slash their arms and legs so that they become caked with dried blood; sometimes the blood is not washed off for many weeks. Widows who wish to make an extravagant display of their bereavement gash themselves fearfully and move off alone to live destitute in the brush. The isolation may last a full year, until relatives begin gradually to camp around them, slowly reincorporating them into kin and community life. In these instances the death of a husband means the almost total severance of social bonds for the survivor. Mourning provides the women with their own masochistic outlet, and it may be this fact along with a feeling of loss that induces their display.

One effect of such mourning is to force the warriors to take pity on the bereaved by organizing a revenge expedition to take a scalp from the enemy tribe that did the killing. The fact that men simply let down their hair in mourning and do not lacerate or isolate themselves reveals that the death of a woman is not felt to be as deep a loss to society as is that of a man; women, in short, are not valued as highly as men. In either case, relatives exhibit their sense of loss for many years; whenever they pass the grave, they keen and wail.

Cheyenne healing rests on two different sets of medical practices. The first takes the form of empirical pharmaceutics and surgery. The second expresses itself in the form of therapeutic thaumaturgy, or curing magic, based upon a specific theory of disease causation.

Either through their own experimentation or by borrowing from others the Cheyenne have come to possess knowledge of some fifty wild plants that have specific properties for the cure or relief of one malaise or another. They constitute remedies for headache, dizziness, constipation and diarrhea, upset stomach, vomiting, kidney trouble, hemorrhage of the lungs and bowels, nosebleed, pus-filled abscesses, poison ivy, snake bite, fever, coughs and colds, sprains and swellings, insufficient lactation, excessive menstrual bleeding, rheumatic pains, paralysis, sore gums, toothache, earache, numbness, and skin irritation; others are tranquilizers and mild, general stimulants. (See Grinnell 1923:II, 169–191 for a detailed identification of Cheyenne medicines.) The medications for these ailments are in the nature of "household" remedies. Some of them are very effective, indeed; all of them are effective to some degree. The Cheyennes know just what part of the plant is to be used in each instance. For internal cures they make effusions in the form of tea. For external applications they make either powders or poultices to be applied directly to the affected part. They have no theory as to what causes the ailments listed above; they just happen. They have no theory as to why particular herbs cure these same diseases; they just do.

In ordinary diseases herbal remedies are the first line of defense. Almost every extended family has some members who know how to prepare and administer most of the drugs known to the Cheyennes. It is the protracted and serious illness, the severe injury that calls for the work of the specialist—the medicine man and his wife. Here we move into theoretical medicine and supernaturalism. The basic Cheyenne assumption concerning serious illness is that it is caused by the intrusion of a tangible foreign object into the body of the person. The object may be one of a number of things: a little ball of hair, a small feather, a bit of crystal, or a thorn. The cure is a ritual performance to locate and dislodge the element, followed by the doctor's sucking on the spot. This results in removal of the object, which is then shown by the doctor to all those in the lodge. Obviously, the effectiveness of such cures lies in their psychological influence. The mystic healing rites are intensive faith cures consisting of psychosomatic therapy, reinforced with sleight-of-hand artistry on the part of the doctor. R. H. Lowie pointed out some time ago that this theoretical assumption (major diseases are things that get into the body and do violence to it in some way) and its accompanying therapeutic conclusion (these things must be gotten out of the body) are distributed among all the tribes east of the Rockies; opposite to this concept is the soul-loss theory of disease—that is, illness is caused by the capturing of the soul by a sorcerer—which predominates west of the Rockies and over into Asia (Lowie 1924:176–180).

Doctors usually purchase their curing rites from older doctors. Sometimes they get them directly in dreams—which simply means that they have watched doctors at work, learned their techniques, subconsciously assimilated them, and then bestowed upon themselves the right to use them by having a supernatural being (animal or bird or anthropomorphic figure) instruct them in dreams or visions.

When practicing, each Cheyenne doctor must be assisted by his wife or some other woman, as are the Pledgers of the major ceremonies.

Not all the work of the Cheyenne healers rests on the intrusion theory. Some of these men are skilled practitioners in dealing with bloody wounds and broken bones by use of direct surgery. These are situations in which a direct mechanical cause is easy to discern; direct, empirically arrived-at techniques are used in response. With effective technical skill, the Cheyennes have no need to fall back on a mystical theoretical concept. They can set even badly broken bones in a rawhide cast and effect totally successful fusions. They can cut out imbedded arrowheads and with astringent drugs stop the bleeding and reduce inflammation. In a few rare instances, however, they are believed to have saved lives by the concentrated use of mystic powers without either sucking or surgery. No explanation is given as to how such cures are brought about other than that birds and animals appear on the scene to work their miraculous effect.

11 / Personality and culture

Reserved and dignified, the mature adult Cheyenne male moves with a quiet sense of self-assurance. He speaks fluently, but never carelessly. He is careful of the sensibilities of others and is kindly and generous. He is slow to anger and strives to suppress his feelings, if aggravated. Vigorous on the hunt and in war, he prizes the active life. Towards enemies he feels no merciful compunctions, and the more aggressive he is, the better. He is well versed in ritual knowledge. He is neither flighty nor dour. Usually quiet, he has a lightly displayed sense of humor. He is sexually repressed and masochistic, but that masochism is expressed in culturally approved rites. He does not show much creative imagination in artistic expression, but he has a firm grip on reality. He deals with the problems of life in set ways while at the same time showing a notable capacity to readjust to new circumstances. His thinking is rationalistic to a high degree and yet colored with mysticism. His ego is strong and not easily threatened. His superego, as manifest in his strong social conscience and mastery of his basic impulses, is powerful and dominating. He is "mature"—serene and composed, secure in his social position, capable of warm social relations. He has powerful anxieties, but these are channeled into institutionalized modes of collective expression with satisfactory results. He exhibits few neurotic tendencies.

Not all, of course, succeed or even have the personality bent to achieve this modal ideal, but during the Climax Period the pressures of Cheyenne enculturation were focused strongly in this direction.

The typical grown-up Cheyenne woman exhibits much the same constellation of traits. Not having the direct outlet for aggressive impulses that men find in war, she is touchier in domestic relations and apt to be a bit willful within her family. Grinnell calls her "masterful." She is more artistically creative than the male, but still within prescribed limits. She is equally repressed sexually but manifests less compensatory behavior in masochism and aggression against enemies—although both these traits are discernible in her.

The molding of the adult, of course, begins in infancy. Cheyenne children are highly valued by their parents and by the tribe. From the outset, their lives are made as comfortable as is possible. They are strictly taught and steadily but gently molded toward the Cheyenne ideal in an atmosphere of love and interest. The Cheyenne child is rarely physically punished, and we have seen how daughters may react in suicide if their mothers are overly harsh or vindictive after they have grown up.

Birth is attended to by the female relatives of the mother assisted by some knowledgeable old midwives. A special birth lodge is sometimes raised, al-

95

Wolf Robe, born 1841. Photo by De Lancey Gill, B.A.E., 1909. (Courtesy the Smithsonian Institution, Bureau of American Ethnology)

Spirit Woman, born 1858. Photo by De Lancey Gill, B.A.E., 1908. (Courtesy the Smithsonian Institution, Bureau of American Ethnology)

though most births take place in the home tipi. The mother in labor does not lie in bed but kneels on a hay-covered robe before a stout frame of poles set firmly in the ground. She seizes a vertical pole and is embraced from the front by a midwife, who braces her own back against the framework. Another midwife receives the baby and removes it from the rear.

As soon as the baby is born, the mother's uvula is tickled to make her gag, thus forcing out the placenta, which is wrapped in a bundle and hung out in a tree. The baby's umbilical cord is cut, tied, and salved. When it finally drops off, it is carefully saved by the mother, dried, and sewed into a little buckskin bag to be kept by the child until it grows up, perhaps well into adulthood. According to the Cheyennes, the navel contains some of the essence of a child's personality, and the child who does not care for its umbilical cord will be disobedient and bad. Except for this belief, there is little of the mystical in Cheyenne birth practices. Mothers, it is true, must observe a few minor prenatal tabus, and a medicine man may be engaged to sing during the birth, but the general tenor of the whole proceeding is one of simple obstetrics. The father may not enter the tipi until after the baby is born; but he is busy with practical tasks outside, keeping the fire going and helping the woman who is cooking a meal for the birth attendants. He engages in no magic, observes no special tabus, nor engages in anything resembling the couvade. Nor is the mother ritually isolated after giving birth. She rests in the tipi for four days, it is true, and during this time her child is wet-nursed, but the idea behind this practice is that she needs rest to regain her strength. There are no purificatory rites before she or her baby may rejoin the society.

Newborn babies are gently greased, powdered, and wrapped in soft robes. If the weather is cold, they are carried in the mother's arms for warmth and comfort. Cheyenne mothers use the cradleboard—a wooden frame carried on the mother's back and on which is a laced-up animal-skin "cocoon" in which the infant is tightly bound like a mummy. The baby is ordinarily not put on the cradleboard until some weeks after its birth. The advantage of its use is that the mother may go about her work with an assurance that her baby will not get into trouble. If traveling, or watching a dance or ceremony, she carries the board like a knapsack; when working in the lodge, she hangs it upright from one of the lodge poles; when working outside the lodge, she leans it against the lodge covering. Although the infant is tightly confined when tied in the cradleboard, this does not retard its development in learning to walk or in other phases of growth. It must early learn quiet patience, however. Crying is not tolerated. The Cheyennes say this is because a squalling baby might give away the camp position at night when enemy raiders are seeking it for an attack. On a deeper level, however, the Cheyennes abhor anyone forcing his will upon others by self-display, and this behavior principle must be learned from the onset. Crying babies are not scolded, slapped, or threatened. They are simply taken out on the cradleboard away from the camp and into the brush where they are hung on a bush. There the squalling infant is left alone until it cries itself out. A few such experiences indelibly teach it that bawling brings not reward but complete and total rejection and the loss of all social contacts. On the other hand, the good baby is cuddled and constantly loved. When not on the board it is rocked in the arms of its mother or grandmother and soothed with lullabies. It is nursed whenever it shows a desire (self-demand feeding).

As the infant gets a little older, it is more often carried about on its mother's back in a blanket sling rather than on the cradleboard. Its head projects about her shoulders; it hears and sees all she does; it shares the warmth of her body and feels the movements of her muscles; it receives food passed over the mother's shoulder; it even sleeps on her back as she goes about her household tasks. It is enveloped in warmth, movement, and affectionate attention. Its body is gently soothed with medicated ointments and soft vegetable ointments. Its early years are full of adult-given gratification. Its frustrations must, however, be quickly internalized, for the alternative is isolation in the brush. This is the first lesson learned, and it must be remembered at all times; it pervades Cheyenne life. (For example, for murderers the penalty is exile from the tribe.) Children are to be quiet and respectful in the presence of elders. The learned have much to offer, and what one acquires in wisdom about the Cheyenne way one acquires through learning taught by those who know the way. Cheyenne relations between younger and elder are thus the relations of pupils and teachers—and pupils must be deferential.

On the basis of this well-established relationship, Cheyenne children are continuously exhorted by their elders: "Be brave, be honest, be virtuous, be industrious, be generous, do not quarrel! If you do not do these things, people will talk about you in the camp; they will not respect you; you will be shamed. If you listen to this advice you will grow up to be a good man or woman, and you will amount to something." The values of the Cheyennes are made explicit in a steady stream of sermonizing that expostulates what is deeply woven into everyday life. The values are reinforced by many explicit mechanisms of public and family approval.

A child does not have to wait until it is grown up to be able to practice what is preached and to experience the satisfaction of performance. Cheyenne children are little replicas of their elders in interests and deeds. Children begin to learn adult activities and practice them in play at incredibly early ages. Boys learn to ride almost as soon as they learn to walk, girls soon after. At two or three, they ride with their mothers, and by the time they are five or six, little boys are riding bareback on their own colts and mastering the use of the lasso. By seven or eight, they help with the herding of the camp's horses. Little girls, as soon as they can toddle, follow their mothers to gather wood and bring in water, the mothers patiently helping them with their pint-sized burdens. Boys get small, but good quality, bows and arrows as soon as they can effectively learn to use them. As Grinnell observed,

> In their hunting, these tiny urchins displayed immense caution and patience, creeping stealthily about through the underbrush of the river bottom, or among the sagebrush on the prairie. . . . The care with which they twisted and wound in and out of cover when approaching the game, taking advantage of every inequality in the ground, of the brush, and of the clumps of ryegrass, was precisely what they would have to practice when hunting in later life (Grinnell 1923:I, 115).

Until they are twelve or thirteen, when they are ready for real hunting and their first war expeditions, the boys join with the girls at "play camp." The girls have small tipis, made for them by their mothers. The boys choose older girls to be their mothers; the smallest children are used as babies, and the routine of full family life is mimicked throughout the day. The boys catch fish and bring in birds and rabbits for their food. They cannot kill real buffalo, but they have great fun with imitation buffalo surrounds. The boys who are the make-believe buffalo carry a prickly pear on a stick to represent the buffalo's horns and heart. They go out first to "graze." Other boys, mounted on sticks, ride out to surround them and charge in with their bows and blunt arrows for the "kill." An arrow in the center of the prickly pear brings down the game; if it is off the center, the "bull" is only wounded and turns and charges to give the unskilled hunter a swat on his rear end with the spiny cactus. War is also played with faithful mimicry of the real thing, including the dismantling of the "camp" by the girls, who flee to safety with their "children" and belongings while their "men" try to stave off the enemy. In the play associated with the children's camps (which, incidentally, they call "large play" in contrast to small girls' and boys' play with dolls and toy bows and arrows, which is called "small play") they even put on Sun Dances. Some of the boys may pierce themselves with cactus thorns and drag chunks of wood, calling them buffalo skulls.

A boy's first real hunt and war party comes early in life—at twelve or thirteen. His first buffalo kill is rewarded with great public recognition, if his family can afford it. His father calls out the news for all in the camp to hear, and he announces that he is giving a good horse—even his best one—to some poor man, in honor of the event. This man gets on the horse to ride all around the camp, signing a song in praise of the boy. The youngster's mother may get up a feast, to which the father publicly invites a number of poor people to share in the family's good fortune. Gifts of blankets and other valuables may be distributed at the end of the feast. The same thing is done when a boy comes home from his first war party.

It is easy to imagine the sense of glowing pride of the young teen-ager who gets such attention on his first manly successes. Cheyenne youths have little reason to be rebels-without-cause. They slip early into manhood, knowing their contributions are immediately wanted, valued, and ostentatiously rewarded. In the family response we see also the signalizing of Cheyenne social consciousness. Some families do better than others, winning more goods and more prestige, but what they have is shared with those who are less able and more luckless. The boy and his parents get tremendous ego-gratification; at the same time, however, they must think of others. Here, too, we see revealed the Cheyenne attitude toward wealth. It is not to be hoarded or to be self-consumed. Stinginess and miserliness are un-Cheyenne. Its value derives from its being given away. Chiefs, who are the greatest exemplars of Cheyenne virtues, are the greatest givers. Note also, that the Cheyennes do not expect an equal return in gifts, except in marriage exchanges; nor is there anything comparable to the Northwest Coast Indian potlatch with its competitive rivalries. Cheyenne boys learn to become highly competitive in the skills of hunt and war. They are rewarded with great individual prestige for successful performance, but the fact is also impressed upon them that they fight for the benefit of the tribe, "to protect the people," and that the fruits of the hunt are to be widely shared.

It is also important to observe that there are no initiation or puberty rites for boys in Cheyenne culture. Cheyenne children acquire full adult status by performance, without the necessity of undergoing hazing by the old men or any other form of *rite de passage*. This fact is illustrated in the timing of the piercing of the ears (pierced ears hold the rings with which the Cheyennes are so fond of adorning themselves). In many parts of the world this event would be part of the puberty ceremonies, and the privilege of wearing the decorations would be an indication of adult status. Not so, with the Cheyennes: ears are ceremonially pierced at the ages of three to six, the action being performed on occasion of the tribal ceremonial gatherings. The honored man who is to pierce a child's ears is sent for by the father through the medium of a crier, who makes the announcement to all the camp. The ear piercer counts coup, performs his task, and receives a munificent present of horses or other goods.

One might say that if there is any initiation for the Cheyenne boy, it takes place on his first warpath:

> . . . in all ways the journey was made easy for them. Yet when the moment came to fight, they were given every opportunity to distinguish themselves. . . . While such little boys did not often accomplish any great feat, yet sometimes they did so, and returned to the village covered with glory, to the unspeakable delight and pride of their families, and to be objects of respect and admiration to their less ambitious and energetic playfellows (Grinnell 1923:I, 122–123).

Such a boy receives a new name, chosen from among those belonging to his family's most outstanding predecessors. He is now, indeed, a full-fledged adult.

For the Cheyenne girl, on the other hand, there is a clear-cut transition rite. Before the time of her menses, however, she, like the boy, receives continuous encouragement and family rewards for her achievements. My own Cheyenne informant, Calf Woman, was seven when her mother started her on her first robe quilling. When she had finished it and placed it over her little baby niece as a present, her grown-up brother said, "Well, I shall have to give her a present to keep her up. She will learn to expect things for her efforts." And he gave her a pony. Later, when a baby girl was born to her brother, Calf Woman beaded a cradleboard for the infant. Her brother gave her a mare.

The first menstruation of a girl is a great event. She has entered womanhood, and her father calls the news to the entire camp from beside his lodge door. If wealthy in horses, he gives one away to signalize the occasion. Like other Indians, the Cheyennes nonetheless consider menstrual blood to be defiling and inimical to the virility of males and to their supernatural powers. The girl therefore retires to an isolation, or moon, hut so that there will be no danger of her polluting her father's or brothers' sacred paraphernalia. Before going, however, she lets down her hair, bathes, and has her body painted all over in red by her older woman relatives. She takes a ceremonial incense purification just before she goes into the hut, where she remains four days with her grandmother, who looks after her and advises her on womanly conduct. At the end of the period, she is again smoked in incense to purify her for reentry into social life. Until menopause, all Cheyenne women leave their tipis for the moon lodge, but only unmarried girls must go through the purification each time.

After her first menses, each girl receives her chastity belt from her mother. She wears it constantly until married. Even after marriage she wears it whenever her husband is away at war or on the hunt. She wears it whenever she goes away from her lodge to gather wood or water. For any man other than her husband to touch it is a private delict of the first magnitude. In one case, a man was nearly stoned to death by the girl and her mother in a surprise ambush. The least that the miscreant may expect is that the girl's female relatives will charge his camp and destroy it. In the one case in which this actually happened, the parents of the guilty boy made no resistance.

Individual assaults with intent to rape are nonexistent among the Cheyenne—except for the case of Bear Rope, who assaulted his daughter. She disemboweled him with a knife while protecting her virtue. The Arrows were renewed for Bear Rope's death, but the daughter was not exiled, for her parricide was justified.

The sexual repression and self-control of the Cheyennes have been sufficiently noted in our previous discussions. Its harmless aggressive outlet in the men's sham attacks on the root diggers has been described (p. 65). Its masochistic expression in the self-aggression of Sun Dance torture and self-sacrifice of flesh and fingers has been detailed. In only one institutionalized practice within the tribe are the floodgates opened to release all the pent-up, subconscious, frustration-bred sexual aggression of the males. This is supposed to take place when a woman is flagrantly adulterous. In the four cases which we were able to record (Llewellyn and Hoebel 1941:202–210) the triggering events were desertion, simple adultery, and refusal to enter into a sororate marriage—all exasperating actions by strong-willed women toward men who claimed a husband's rights. The response is to "put a woman on the prairie," called noha's3w3stan (literally "any man's wife"). The outraged husband invites all the unmarried members of his military society (excepting his wife's relatives) to a feast on the prairie. There the woman is raped by each of them in turn. Big Footed Woman was forced into intercourse with forty or more of her husband's confreres when a young wife. She survived it and lived to be a hundred, but no one ever married her afterwards. Tassel Woman was nearly dead when she was rescued by Blue Wing and his wife. The right of a husband to give his wife to his soldier "brothers" is not denied, yet it is a formal right that the Cheyennes in fact cannot accept with equanimity. In two cases, the brothers and father of the woman went forth to attack the whole soldier band, threatening to shoot to kill regardless of the ban on murder. The soldiers scattered and kept out of their way. In the case of Little Sea Shell, the girl fled to the wife of the Keeper of the Holy Hat, for the band was on the march and the Hat Keeper's wife had the Buffalo Hat Bundle on her back at the time. The lodge of the Hat Keeper is an asylum in which even an enemy raider may find sanctuary. If he can get to the Holy Hat Lodge, he is immune and will be escorted safely out of Cheyenne country. In this instance, the Hat Keeper's wife made a symbolic lodge by putting her arms about Little Sea Shell while holding a stick associated with the Hat Bundle. Her quick thinking saved the girl.

Men who have participated in a gang rape are not proud of it. The women in the camps taunt them, and they do not defend themselves; they just hang their heads and walk away. Clearly, the deed runs counter to dominant Cheyenne values. We suspect that the right of the husband to do this to his wife is very old and may have some sacred significance. Grinnell mentions that just before the great fight with the Pawnees and Potawatomi, in 1853, Long Chin was putting on the Holy Hat to wear in the battle when the chin strap broke. This was very bad luck, so to counteract it Long Chin "publicly pledged himself to give a woman to be passed on the prairie" (Grinnell 1915:88). The deed may originally have had some of the quality of the action in which the wife of a Pledger of one of the great ceremonies is offered to the

High Priest or Instructor. In any event, the practice is an anomaly in terms of Cheyenne ideals, but understandable in terms of psychodynamics.

According to formal belief, any woman who has been four times divorced becomes a "free woman" —any man's game. Although there is no memory of this ever having happened, one of the four Virgins of the Elk Soldiers was once put on this footing because she had lost her virginity before marriage. The Elks cut her hair and turned her loose, publicly disgraced. No man would marry her, although many went to her for intercourse. She was really a kind of outlaw—like the banished Sticks-Everything-Under-His-Belt. But, like him, she was rehabilitated and reinstated in the tribe by a Sun Dance pledged in her honor, sometime around 1865. In the Sun Dance, the priest prayed to Maiyun to give her a new life, and when it was over, the Pledger married her. Like the earth, she was renewed, and she lived faultlessly with her husband for many years.

Finally, the inversion of Cheyenne personality in the Contraries needs to be examined in the present context. It will be remembered that a small handful of men reject the male warrior role by becoming transvestites. Others, the Contraries, overdo the warrior role in an institutionalized form of extreme exaggeration. The first important fact is that the Contraries may not marry. If they do, they must give up their lances and behave like normal people. The second fact is that the Contraries court death with extreme recklessness in battle; their lances give them "great luck," however, and they are hard to kill. We put these two facts together and suggest the following: the Contraries, like the Halfmen-halfwomen, are neurotically anxious about sex relations and their own virility. Whereas the Halfmen-halfwomen find their refuge in total rejection of male sexuality, the Contraries seek validation in an exaggerated male rejection of heterosexuality.

The symbol of the Contrary is the Thunder Bow, a special bow decorated with magic feathers and bearing a lancehead on one end. An ordinary lance is a perfectly good weapon that may or may not be endowed with sexual symbolism. The Thunder Bow is not a weapon, however. It is carried in battle, but it is used only to count coup. It is significant that its point may not touch the earth—the bearer of life, the essence of femininity. Symbolically, the Thunder Bow suggests the male sex organ tied and restrained.

Two further facts that demonstrate the sexual implications of this status are, first, that a Contrary may never sit or lie upon a bed and, second, that man becomes a Contrary because "he is afraid of thunder and lightning." He dreams that he must become a Contrary and that this will cure him of his anxiety. The Thunder-bird, from whom the Contraries' great supernatural power comes, is a male figure.

In his rejection of heterosexuality, the Contrary rejects normal social relations. He must live alone, apart from all the camp. Whatever he does in social relations he does backwards. Ask him to do one thing and he will do its opposite. Even in battle, he cannot charge with the other warriors at his side, or in front or behind him. He must be off on the flanks, alone. When he holds his Thunder Bow in his right hand, he may not retreat.

The Contrary, then, is the Cheyenne warrior male with a monomania for what might be called military virility. For this, he is highly respected—and pitied. The Cheyennes say it is a fearsome and difficult thing to be a Contrary, an almost unbearable burden. Contrariness may be seen as providing a customary outlet through which extreme cases of anxiety are turned constructively to the social benefit of a warrior nation. Yet, if it were allowed to spread throughout the society, it would rend the social fabric. This threat is mastered by limiting the number of Contraries to two or three. A man may become a Contrary only by purchasing the Thunder Bow and power of one who is already a Contrary. The seller is then released of his obligations and may marry and return to normal life.

In summing up this study of Cheyenne life in the high period of their independent life on the Plains, the following points must be mentioned. The Cheyennes stand out among the nomadic Indians of the Plains for their dignity, chastity, steadfast courage, and tightly structured, yet flexible, social organization. Never a large tribe, they have held their own with outstanding success. They have come to terms with their environment and with themselves. They are exceedingly rational and skilled in cultural adaptation through felicitous social inventiveness and manipulation. Although deep down they are beset with anxieties, their anxieties are institutionally controlled. Their adaptation to the Plains way of life was sudden and rapid. In this situation of flux they have faced three great threats: famine, enemies, and internal disruption. They ward off famine with carefully police-controlled group hunting, abetted by occasional supernaturally directed group hunts, and they constantly reassure themselves by tribal World Renewal ceremonies. They hold off their enemies by exaltation of the military life combined with a system of firm alliances with selected neighboring tribes. They counter the forces of internal disruption (in part engendered by the training values necessary to successful war making) by repression of sex, by vesting authority in those who are learned, by organized government and removal of tribal chiefs from status competition, by emphasis on altruism, by banishment of murderers, and by reinforcement of tribal unity through the great tribal ceremonies. Reasonably effective mechanisms for intrasocietal release of aggressive tensions are provided in mock battles between men and women, in a variety of competitive games, in self-torture, and in institutionalized role transfers for a few of the men.

The major basic postulates underlying Cheyenne culture of the Climax Period, and therefore dominant in the control of Cheyenne behavior, are as follows:

POSTULATE I. The world (universe) is fundamentally a mechanical system with a limited energy quotient which progressively diminishes as it is expended.

POSTULATE II. The energy quotient of the world is rechargeable through compulsive mimetic acts of sympathetic ritual.

Corollary 1. Ritual officiants must learn the exact formulas of world renewal from knowledgeable experts.

Corollary 2. Acts are more effective than words.

POSTULATE III. Human beings are subordinate to supernatural forces and spirit beings. These forces and beings have superior knowledge concerning the operation of the universe and are benevolently inclined toward mankind.

Corollary 1. Tribal well-being and individual success are abetted by the tutelage or blessing of the supernaturals.

Corollary 2. Prayer, pledges, and self-sacrifice win the attention and help of the supernaturals.

POSTULATE IV. The social order is fragile and threatened by aggressive tendencies in Cheyenne character.

Corollary 1. All first obligations are to the maintenance of the well-being of the tribe.

Corollary 2. All aggressive behavior within the tribe is dangerous and bad.

POSTULATE V. The authority of the tribal council is derived from the supernaturals and is supreme over all other elements in the society.

POSTULATE VI. The killing of a Cheyenne by a Cheyenne pollutes the tribal fetishes and the murderer.

Corollary 1. Bad luck will dog the tribe until the fetishes are purified.

Corollary 2. Murderers may not be killed but must be separated from the social body through banishment.

POSTULATE VII. Sex interests generate jealousy and hostility; they must be held to a minimum.

Corollary 1. Chastity and abstinence are good.

Corollary 2. Marriage among relatives is impossible.

POSTULATE VIII. Sex relations are necessary for procreation and regenerative ritual.

Corollary 1. Women must officially participate in religious rituals and in curing.

POSTULATE IX. War is necessary to defend and advance the interests of the tribe.

POSTULATE X. War is necessary to permit individual self-expression and personality development of the male.

POSTULATE XI. The virility of men, like the energy of the world, is limited.

Corollary 1. Male genitals must be magically protected.

Corollary 2. Abstinence conserves male energy for war.

POSTULATE XII. Men are more important than women.

Corollary 1. The husband is the head of the household.

Corollary 2. All governmental posts are held by men.

POSTULATE XIII. Children (excluding infants) have the same qualities as adults; they lack only in experience.

Corollary 1. Children should, on their level, engage in adult activities.

Corollary 2. Children become adults as soon as they are physically able to perform adult roles.

POSTULATE XIV. All land, and the tribal fetishes, are public property.

POSTULATE XV. All other material goods are private property, but they should be generously shared with others.

POSTULATE XVI. The individual personality is important.

Corollary 1. The individual must be permitted and encouraged to express his potentiality with the greatest possible freedom compatible with group existence.

Corollary 2. Rehabilitation of delinquents and criminals after punishment is extremely important.

These principles form the bedrock upon which the Cheyennes have raised their cultural edifice, which is for them The Cheyenne Way.

PART THREE Postlude (1850–1978)

12 / War with the United States (1856–1879)

As long as the plains were visited only by traders, occasional explorers, and travelers, the Cheyennes had no armed conflicts with the whites or with the United States Government.

In the 1840s, however, relations with the whites began to undergo a drastic change. Oregon was open to settlement as American territory. The first party of settlers from the East passed up the Platte River, through the heart of the Northern Cheyenne hunting grounds in 1841. They were not claiming any Cheyenne or Sioux land, but their presence was disturbing to the game. Their horses, cattle, and wagons offered the possibility for a little loot; wagon trains were occasionally robbed, and often they were stopped and subjected to demands for coffee, tobacco, and other "pay-offs." From Oregon a cry went back to the East for protection on the Emigrant Road.

The United States Government responded. Fort Kearney was built and garrisoned two hundred miles up the Platte River in Nebraska. Another fort, Laramie, was established far out in the plains, at the foot of the Rocky Mountains, six hundred miles up the road from its starting point. The stage for war was being set.

First Oregon; then California. When gold was discovered in 1849, twenty thousand fortune seekers hurried through the Cheyenne country on their way to the West Coast. With them they brought cholera, a hideous disease which killed nearly half the Cheyenne people in a few summer months. One can easily imagine its terrifying and unsettling effect. Two bands, the Poor People and the Bare Shins, were wholly wiped out. A third, the Flexed Legs, was so reduced that its survivors joined Porcupine Bear's camp of Dog Soldiers. The long Cheyenne struggle for survival was precariously close to being lost.

The remaining Cheyennes found themselves confronted by yet another disturbing condition. The United States took over all Mexican territory north of the Rio Grande after the War with Mexico. Traffic on the Santa Fe Trail, which ran right through the Southern Cheyenne heartland, was increased many times.

THE FORT LARAMIE TREATY: 1851

With the need for a safe link between the eastern states and the newly-acquired territories in the Southwest and along the Pacific Coast, the United States determined to stabilize the situation on the western plains by bringing

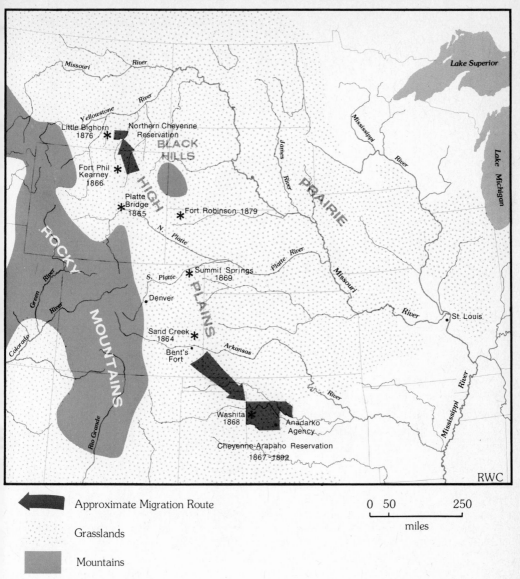

Approximate Migration Route

Grasslands

Mountains

*   Major Battles

Cheyenne battles with the United States, 1856–1879, and the move to reservations.

an end to intertribal wars and securing tribal consent for the free and unmolested passage of emigrant and freight trains.

The physically weakened southern bands of Cheyenne were quite willing to
join with the Arapaho, Crow, Wind River Shoshone, western Sioux, Crow,
Assiniboine, Hidatsa and Arikara in the mid-summer of 1851 to meet with
United States treaty commissioners at Fort Laramie, Wyoming. The Coman-

White Hawk. Photo by L.A. Huffman, Fort Keogh, Montana Territory, 1879
(Courtesy of the Minnesota Historical Society)

che, Kiowa, and Kiowa-Apache tribes refused, for their part, to have anything
to do with the undertaking.

The treaty-making was a spectacular event which lived long in the memory
of all who participated. Ten thousand Indians, with thousands of horses,
gathered in the vicinity of the fort. There were parades of warriors in full
regalia (four thousand Sioux riding four abreast; several hundred Cheyennes in
their own martial display), all-night dances, intertribal hosting at ceremonial

feasts, exchanges of gifts, and mutual adoption of each other's children among the tribes.

Negotiations between the United States representatives and the chiefs of the tribes lasted only nine days. For the Cheyennes, the important provisions of the Fort Laramie Treaty were:

1. The Southern Arapaho and Cheyenne bands merged in a single legal entity for the purposes of treating with the United States. The Northern Cheyenne bands were, in effect, split off as though they formed a separate tribe altogether.

2. The boundaries of the jointly held Southern Cheyenne-Arapaho tribal territory were specified. They embraced all the land between the Arkansas and North Platte Rivers, extending from well into western Kansas and Nebraska to the top of the front range of the Rocky Mountains. They contained much prime hunting country and covered 122,500 square miles, or about 51,000,000 acres, equal to approximately 8,000 acres per man, woman, and child.

This was not a reservation. It was Cheyenne-Arapaho territory, which all signatory tribes and the United States mutually agreed to respect as such.

3. The Cheyenne-Arapaho gave permission to the United States to build and maintain roads through their territory, and to establish and garrison such forts as were deemed necessary. In other words, the tribes agreed to legalize the extra-territorial privileges which the United States had already preempted.

4. In compensation for these privileges, the United States agreed to pay the tribes $50,000 annually for ten years. Annuities of food and clothing would be delivered to the tribes, according to the judgment of the President. Farm animals and tools would also be given to help the Indians resume the sedentary farming they had given up when they turned to nomadic hunting three generations earlier.

5. The Indian nations bound themselves to make restitution for any acts of wrongdoing by their people against any people of the United States *lawfully* residing in, or passing through, their territory.

6. The United States guaranteed to protect the signatory Indian nations from all depredations by the people of the United States.

The Treaty of Fort Laramie was filled with good—but wholly unrealistic—intentions. Neither side could possibly, under the prevailing circumstances, enforce the provisions of points five and six.

WAR: PHASE I (1856–1861)

Two years after the Fort Laramie Treaty, in 1853, fifteen thousand Americans in covered wagons lumbered past the fort, destroying game as they went. The Commissioner of Indian Affairs reported that the Cheyenne and Arapaho, as well as the western Sioux, were "actually in a *starving state* . . . Their women are pinched with want and their children constantly crying out with hunger."

Small wonder that parties of warriors harassed the wagon trains with demands for food, tobacco, and trinkets. Frightened emigrants responded with demands for aggressive action from the troops stationed along the way.

For the Cheyenne, the war began in 1856. A small group of Cheyennes, who were part of a large war party directed against the Pawnee, frightened the driver of a mail coach, who shot at them and, in return, received an arrow wound. The next morning, a troop of cavalry from Fort Kearney charged the nearby Indian camp, killing or wounding eighteen Cheyennes.

The Cheyennes immediately retaliated. They attacked two wagon trains, killing a United States official, the Secretary for Utah Territory, and a half-dozen other men, women, and children.

The pattern had been set for mutual genocide. A few Indians might make an aggressive act. Swift military punishment would fall on the heads of other Indians, guilty or not. Outraged tribesmen, usually the younger warriors, would retaliate by falling on innocent pioneers and settlers. Sometimes warriors would meet troopers in battle.

After the affair near Fort Kearney, the Cheyennes and the United States prepared for war. Two Cheyenne medicine men worked up a supernatural power which they believed would cause bullets to drop harmlessly from the muzzles of the Army's guns. On the other side, the U.S. Army sent out a strong striking force of cavalry, infantry, and artillery. This expedition found itself suddenly confronted by several hundred Cheyenne warriors in battle array, late in July of 1857. Quite by chance, Colonel Leavenworth, the commander, ordered an all-out sabre-charge without firing a shot. The Cheyenne warriors, expecting to face only guns which would not work, were unnerved and routed. Few were killed, but their entire camp was destroyed, their annuities confiscated, and their faith in the power of their sacred beliefs badly damaged.

In the years ahead, the Cheyenne would taste the fruits of victory in several pitched battles, but the theme of their military doom was set.

Gold in the Rockies: 1858   The Cheyennes had known for some time that there was gold in the gravels of the rivers that flowed out of the Rockies and into the plains. They had no interest in it for themselves, but they knew full well what had caused the stampede of travelers through their country during the gold rush of '49. One old chief told their friend, the trader William Bent, ". . . if the white men ever found the gold they would take from the Cheyennes their 'best and last home' " (Lavender 1954:337). In 1858, the cat escaped the bag. Gold in the Rockies! A new rush was on. An estimated hundred thousand hopeful searchers poured through and into the Cheyenne-Arapaho country, the slogan "Pike's Peak or Bust" painted on the canvas of many of their covered wagons. Towns such as Pueblo, Denver, Boulder, and Colorado City—plus dozens of mining camps—were built to supply and maintain the forty thousand whites who stayed through the winter of 1859–60. All were illegal invaders under the provisions of the Fort Laramie Treaty of 1851.

In the United States Senate, Steven A. Douglas, Lincoln's antagonist in the great slavery debates of 1858, declared, "Every man in Pike's Peak is there in violation of law; every man of them has incurred the penalty of $1,000 fine and six months' imprisonment for going in violation of the Indian intercourse law," and claiming land which was under Indian title (Hafen 1974:141).

What could the United States Government do about it? Send in the army to drive out its citizens and burn down their towns? Hardly a realistic possibility, either politically or in practical military terms. The edifice of mutual accommodation agreed upon at Laramie only nine years before was a shambles.

The trader, William Bent, acting as Indian Agent for the government, strove to stabilize the situation while prodding Congress and the Federal Administration to negotiate a new treaty in which the Indians would cede the lands occupied by the Colorado towns, plus strips along the roadways. The government would guarantee the Indians adequate annuities to replace the vanishing buffalo and, above all, assure them that without fail all the rest of their territory would be closed forever to white intrusion. Failing this, wrote Bent, "A smothered passion for revenge agitates these Indians, perpetually fermented by the failure of food, the encircling encroachments of the white population, and *the exasperating sense of decay and impending extinction with which they are surrounded. . . . A desperate war of starvation and extinction is imminent and inevitable, unless prompt measure shall prevent it* (italics added: Lavender 1954:343).

The Fort Wise Treaty: 1861   The United States' response to the desperate situation of the Southern Cheyennes and Arapahos was to negotiate a new treaty at Fort Wise.

The treaty accepted the occupation of the western part of the Cheyenne-Arapaho country by the miners as an accomplished fact which would not be undone. Therefore, it provided that:

1. The tribes relinquished (ceded) to the United States all the land which had been specified as theirs only ten years before—except for a much smaller reserved area.
2. The United States agreed to pay $450,000 for the land given up.
3. The United States would build and maintain flour mills, saw mills, and a machine shop to maintain farm implements.
4. Individual ownership of tax-free farms was provided for.
5. The reservation would be closed to all white persons except government employees and government-licensed traders.

The treaty marked a change in the government's policy toward the Cheyennes. The Treaty of Fort Laramie had assumed that the Indians could continue their previous hunting existence indefinitely—so long as they did not make war on whites. The Treaty of Fort Wise was based on the premise that times were changing and that the Indians would simply have to alter their mode of subsistence. They must settle down as farmers, and the government would help them to do it.

The treaty also signalled the decay of the old-time governmental system of the Cheyenne tribe. Most of the tribe, including the military society chiefs, were off on the annual summer hunt while the treaty was being negotiated. Six Peace Chiefs, acting on their own, presumed to sign the treaty without consultation in the usual way. They simply felt that there was no choice but to set aside the past and adjust to the future as farmers. The alternative was war to the death for the Cheyennes as a people. That they wished to avoid.

The Dog Soldier band, however, refused to acknowledge the treaty, and others likewise ignored it, so it was never even tried out. All Cheyennes absolutely refused to move in to the reservation. They were not yet ready to be fenced in.

Following the Fort Wise Treaty Council, the Cheyenne Peace Chiefs managed to keep the young warriors under restraint. Except for sporadic raids on the stagecoach routes for fun and booty, relations between Cheyennes and the Americans remained relatively quiet throughout the early years of the Civil War. The War Chiefs, for their part, tried to turn the energies of their younger followers to making war on their traditional enemies, the Ute Indians, who lived in the Rocky Mountains and beyond. This was ignored by the United States, which was now deep in the struggle for its own national survival.

WAR: PHASE II (1864–1878)

The relative peace after Fort Wise proved in the end to be only a lull in the eye of the hurricane. Nothing had really been settled, only suspended.

In the summer of 1862, frustrated Sioux Indians in the Minnesota River valley, where the Cheyennes had so briefly lived toward the end of the seventeenth century, had gone on a terrible rampage. In a seven-week reign of terror, they destroyed most of the farms in the valley and killed over three hundred and fifty settlers. One hundred and twenty-six soldiers, badly needed on the battlefields in the South, had died in putting down the outbreak. Settlers farther west became almost paranoid in their anxiety for their own safety.

The war parties moving against the Utes had to pass through, or close to, the Colorado towns that lay along the east face of the Rockies. Occasionally, they helped themselves to beef and horses. Mexican traders were plying the young braves with too much whiskey.

Left largely to his own resources, because of Federal concern with the Civil War, the territorial governor in Denver tried to interest the Cheyennes and Arapahos in yet another treaty which would give the white residents of the territory legal title to the lands which they now held as squatters, and which would clear the western reaches of the high plains of Indians by binding them to the proposed reservation in Kansas and Nebraska. No Cheyennes were interested.

In late 1863, Governor Evans gave up on his treaty proposals as a means to achieve peace, and turned instead to war plans.

The leaders of the Cheyenne, Arapaho, and Sioux could see what was coming. Throughout the ensuing winter, they held council after council among themselves to plan a coordinated effort to drive the whites off the plains entirely.

The war was opened by the Indians on a small scale in the spring of 1864. Using traditional methods (namely, war parties organized by individuals), they raided stock herds and pillaged ranches and stagecoach stations. Small army detachments would then sally out on forays in search of Indians to punish. Tensions, destruction, and killings began to mount on both sides.

Finally, the torch was applied to the powder keg. Unidentified Indians murdered and atrociously mutilated a farmer, his wife, and children, living near Denver. Coloradans panicked.

In Denver, the Colorado militia was organized and expanded. Volunteers were mostly from the mining camps. Both Governor Evans and the United States military commander set a policy directing their actions only against hostile bands of Indians. Governor Evans informed the peacefully inclined band chiefs to move their peoples' camps to certain designated places close to various army posts. Those who refused to come in would be treated as hostiles and subject to attack.

In mid-July, the Indians launched a widespread and well-coordinated offensive of hit-and-run raids directed against the stock herds of ranches and posts along the branches of the Platte River. They destroyed and looted wagon trains and stagecoaches. Dozens of white civilians were killed, scalped, mutilated, or captured. Using guerrilla-like tactics, raiders and their base camps melted away into the vast plains when military counteraction was undertaken. Colorado was entirely cut off from the rest of the country.

In late summer, peace overtures were made by the Cheyenne Peace Chiefs, Black Kettle and White Antelope, and sympathetically entertained by the commanding field officer in their area, Major Edward Wyncoop. But communications were poor and clashes between war parties and the army continued elsewhere. Major General Curtis, back in Kansas, determined that he wanted no peace until the Indians had been militarily chastised. Lulled by the reasonableness of Major Wyncoop and Indian Agent Cooley, with whom they were negotiating in the field, a number of the Cheyenne and Arapaho band chiefs brought their people into camps on Sand Creek, near Fort Lyon in southeastern Colorado. The summer of terror on the plains seemed to have run its course.

This was not to be. Governor Evans abandoned his policy of distinction between "friendly" and "hostile" Indians. He had now concurred with Curtis' position that the tribes must be smashed. So convinced, he left for Washington to petition for more troops and arms. This left the soon-to-be-notorious Colonel John M. Chivington, commander of the Colorado militia, on his own. Chivington decided on a winter campaign of search and kill. He would strike the Cheyennes where they could most easily be found, resting in false security at Sand Creek. Chivington forced his seven hundred men through snow and cold, in deep secrecy, to appear in battle array before Black Kettle's camp at daybreak on the morning of November 29, 1864. The American flag raised above Black Kettle's tipi offered no sanctuary. With cannons, rifles, and sabers, Chivington's volunteers attacked without warning, and went berserk. Fleeing Cheyennes fought desperately throughout the day. Women and infants, as well as fighters, were slaughtered without mercy. Their bodies were scalped and mutilated with savage atrocity. Some two hundred Cheyennes (the exact number was never established) died on that black day in American history. Two-thirds of them were women and children.

Black Kettle survived the massacre, but White Antelope and eight other leading Cheyenne chiefs died at Sand Creek, plus an undetermined number of lesser band chiefs. Chivington, in one stroke, had wiped out the leaders of the peace faction (mostly members of the Council of Peace Chiefs) among the Southern Cheyennes. The balance of power among the remnants of the tribal government was now shifted to the War Chiefs of the Military Societies.

Black Kettle, thirsting for revenge, went north to join the Dog Soldiers, as did the two half-Cheyenne, half-white sons of William Bent. Filled with burning hatred for the whites, they became ferocious fighters and strategists in the forays that were to come.

Chivington's triumph, as he and the Coloradans saw it, was short-lived. He was forced to resign from the army, and the United States offered to pay sizable indemnities to the kin of the Cheyennes who had died at Sand Creek. The Cheyennes, for their part, were not interested in hand-outs. They thirsted for revenge and blood. As for goods—cattle, horses, food, clothing, and money—they would take what they wanted. And they did.

The Dog Soldier band, now numbering about a hundred warriors and their families, had continued through the years to live apart from other Cheyennes, semi-exiles in northwestern Kansas. The shattered Southern Cheyennes moved north to join them. Sioux and Northern Arapahos responded readily to Cheyenne proposals for a coordinated war on the Platte River lifeline to the far western territories. By New Year, 1865, two thousand warriors, with their camps of families, were gathered along the banks of the Republican River, which straddles the Kansas-Nebraska border for much of its distance.

From early January through the spring and summer of the last year of the Civil War, huge war parties of five hundred to one thousand men attacked up and down the Platte River. Julesberg, Colorado was looted and burned to the ground. Trading posts and stagecoach stations suffered similar fates. Emigrant and wagon trains carrying freight were destroyed. Thousands of cattle and horses were run off. Ranches were put to the torch, their inhabitants killed, scalped, or captured. Telegraph lines were torn down. Indians, who had starved for some years, were living high on white men's provisions.

The handful of troops who had not been drawn off to fight in the East, could in no way cope with the situation. They suffered severe defeats whenever they ventured out from the safety of their forts. At Fort Phil Kearney, an entire command under Colonel W. J. Fetterman was annihilated when he led his men into a set ambush.

The Treaty of the Little Arkansas: 1865   In the spring of 1865, hostilities quieted down. The Cheyenne and Sioux wished to enjoy the fruits of their victory, so they moved off toward the Black Hills to hunt. The government was locked in an internal struggle over what policy to pursue. The generals wanted to mount heavy campaigns to subdue the tribes, at whatever cost. Lee had surrendered at Appomattox. There were now troops and supplies available in great surplus. Even so, Congress and the Bureau of Indian Affairs pressed for a negotiated peace.

A third treaty between the United States and some of the Southern Cheyenne was the outcome; the Treaty of the Little Arkansas was signed on October 14, 1865. More land was ceded by the Cheyenne and Arapaho. All of the territory which had been acknowledged as theirs in the Treaty of Fort Laramie was relinquished. Each Cheyenne who settled on the reservation would receive a small per capita payment for up to forty years.

The Southern Cheyennes and Arapahos were to squeeze into a small reservation in Oklahoma, while the Northern Cheyennes could roam free. Although ratified by the United States Senate, the treaty was never acknowledged or signed by more than a few Cheyenne chiefs. It was only a paper footnote in the continuing struggle to find a working balance between the irresistible westward expansion of the Euro-American population and the need to maintain vestigial hunting areas for the nomadic Plains tribes.

The End of the Civil War: 1865   With the Civil War ended, the major energies of the United States were directed toward industrialization and the settlement of its territories "from sea to shining sea."

Before the Civil War, it had been a question of whether or not wagon trains might be allowed to pass through Indian territory; now the question was whether the tribes would suffer the transcontinental railroads to be built.

And the settlers! Before the War, except for the mining settlements in Colorado, the goal of most overland pioneers lay not in the territory of the

Plains tribes, but in California and Oregon. Now they would be demanding the old hunting grounds themselves for farms and ranches.

In 1800, at the beginning of the Climax Period of the Cheyenne way of life, the total population of the United States was just over five million. At the time of the Fort Laramie Treaty (1851), it was already at twenty-four million. When the Civil War ended, despite the loss of a million Americans, the national population had increased to thirty-six million. By the time the Cheyennes had finally and irrevocably lost their war against the United States, they faced a country of fifty million.

Much of the increase was through native-born Americans, white and black. The rest was the product of a tidal wave of European poor seeking freedom from want and political oppression. A million Irish refugees from famine arrived in the United States in just eight years (1847–1854). Three million German workers found refuge in the United States in the decade following the failure of the German Socialist Revolution of 1848. In all, seven and a half million Europeans crossed the Atlantic, to find a new life in the United States in the first two-thirds of the nineteenth century. Three million more arrived in the fifteen years following the Civil War.

What hope was there for five thousand Cheyennes, twenty thousand Sioux, and a few thousand each of Arapahos, Comanches, Kiowas, Crows, Utes, and others, to carry a defensive war to an ultimate victory?

The Cheyennes had been fighting just such a war for two hundred years. Two factors were different now. There was no longer an open Indian frontier beyond which they could flee and, further, the resources of their new enemy were overwhelming.

Much is made these days of the "Trail of Broken Treaties." In fact, every treaty between the Cheyenne-Arapaho and the United States was invalidated by circumstances within months of its signing. Neither the United States Government nor the leaders of the Indian tribes were capable of controlling the actions of their own people. In international law, a treaty which is broken by one party or the other is automatically invalidated. Both the Cheyennes and the United States broke their treaty commitments. Which party defaulted first is not always clear.

The Treaty of Medicine Lodge Creek: 1867   There was to be one more attempt at finding a treaty solution to the Southern Cheyenne problem. Congress established a blue-ribbon commission of four civilians and three generals to meet with the Cheyenne-Arapaho leaders. The council was held in Kansas in the fall of 1867.

The treaty which was worked out expressed the same basic principles as the ill-fated Treaty of the Little Arkansas. Only the specifics differed:

1. The Cheyenne-Arapaho "tribe" gave up title to all its previously owned land, excepting a new reservation area in what is now Oklahoma.

2. The United States agreed to pay a half million dollars in cash, plus annuities in clothing and food, as necessary, for a period of twenty-five years. It would also provide the services of a resident agent, physician, blacksmith, and school teachers.

3. Heads of families could receive individual allotments of farm lands.

4. The Cheyennes promised to be peaceful and cease all raids on American installations and persons.

This treaty was signed by fourteen Cheyenne chiefs, both Peace Chiefs and War Chiefs.

The treaty did not forbid the Cheyennes from making war on other tribes. So now, instead of going after the Utes, they turned their attention to the Kaw, near neighbors to the east of them.

The war expedition of younger Cheyenne fighters against the Kaw resulted in disappointment. The raiders vented their frustration by burning houses of half-white Kaws while passing through Council Bluffs, Kansas. They also helped themselves to cattle from farms in the vicinity, which had been left deserted in fear of the Cheyenne war party.

Within a week of the issue of a sizable stock of arms and munitions to the Cheyenne by Bureau of Indian Affairs officers, a large war party of Cheyennes, mostly Dog Soldiers, went on a rampage against Kansas settlers. Fired in part by whiskey, which they found when looting ranches, they burned buildings, killed men and women, captured children, and ran off stock—and forced the abandonment of a large area of country.

The Battles of the Washita and Summit Springs: 1868–1869   It was now to be war to the finish. General William T. Sherman—he who had marched through Georgia, fighting and burning as he went—was in command for the United States. As Sherman saw it, the Cheyennes and their allies had to be brought to their knees in a hurry or American settlement of the west forgotten, at least for the near future. The time for parleying had played out.

With small, mobile forces, General Phil Sheridan, in the field, kept the Cheyenne camps on the move throughout the summer and fall of 1868. Then with larger forces at hand, he prepared for a winter campaign at a time when the Indians would be huddled in their camps and movement more difficult for them.

A three-pronged campaign brought Colonel George A. Custer's column of seven hundred men to Black Kettle's village, which was attacked at dawn on November 29th. Black Kettle himself was among a score of Cheyenne and Arapaho fighters who were killed that day—plus twenty to forty women and children. Custer's losses were equal to those of the Indian warriors. Reinforcements from nearby Indian camps induced Custer to break off the attack and withdraw from the field after burning the camp and capturing a large part of its stores, along with nearly a thousand horses. The loss of horses, food, and shelter was a severe blow to the already ill-fed Southern Cheyennes. The Battle of the Washita, as it is called, at last broke their will to resist. One month later, on New Year's Eve, 1868, nineteen chiefs plodded in to Fort Cobb, their horses too weak to carry them. They offered total surrender; their people had no resources or strength with which to carry on.

The Dog Soldier Band, for its part, stubbornly refused to capitulate. It drifted toward its old haunts in north Kansas, where it was joined by a number of diehard Sioux. These five hundred intractable warriors and their families chose to fight to the finish.

With guerrilla tactics, the Dogs killed settlers along the Kansas frontier, took a few women as prisoners, and tore up the tracks of the Kansas Pacific Railroad. In their first brush with pursuing troops, they lost a twentieth of their fighting strength. Two weeks later, the Dog Soldiers were caught in camp while waiting to escape across the South Platte River into Sioux country. One hundred and fifty Pawnee scouts and eight companies of cavalry hit them at a place called Summit Springs in Colorado. Fifty more Dog Soldiers died that day and all their lodges and goods, including food, were destroyed.

Some Dog Soldiers escaped to the Sioux. Others came south in straggling groups to surrender.

The Battle of the Little Bighorn: 1876   The scene of conflict now shifted northward. The Northern Cheyenne bands lived and hunted well north of the emigrant traffic routes which had involved their southern compatriots in so many difficulties. Nor was their country as yet attracting frontier settlers.

Then, in 1874, prospectors who tagged along with Custer's expedition of military reconnaissance, found gold in the Black Hills. In 1875 another rush was on. The Sioux resisted the incursion and miners were attacked and killed. Thus the War of 1876 began.

General George Crook, with a strong column of cavalry and infantry, fought an indecisive battle on the Rosebud River in Montana in mid-June.

A week later, Custer and the Seventh Cavalry found a trail which led to a huge encampment of Cheyennes and Sioux on the Little Bighorn River in Montana. A thousand to fifteen hundred lodges housed two to five thousand fighting men and their families.

Custer was under the command of General Alfred Terry, who was moving up the Yellowstone River with a force of three thousand infantry, cavalry, and a battery of gattling guns. Custer put his troops through a forced march to strike the combined Indian villages before Terry could reach them. He wished all the glory for himself. On June 25, 1876, he attempted a three-pronged attack on the village from above and below. The cavalry assault failed to panic the Indians. Custer's column retreated to high ground where it was pinned down and annihilated to a man. The other two columns under Major Reno and Captain Benteen held out atop a ridge until the middle of the next day, when news of the approach of Terry's strong force caused the Indians to break off the fight and hastily decamp.

Two hundred and sixty-four troopers had died with Custer—not many compared to the seven thousand Federals lost in a single day at Spottsylvania in the Civil War—but enough to make it an exhilarating victory for the Sioux and Northern Cheyenne. Yet they had little time to savor it. The country was swarming with troops, so the allied Indians broke up into small bands, and scattered.

The Capture of Morning Star's Village: 1876   As ever, winter brought hard times for the tribes. Camps had to settle down in protected valleys and food was hard to get. They did not like to make war in the winter.

Winter campaigns were hard on the American soldiers, too. But they could take to the field unencumbered by women and children. With large baggage trains they could stay out in force for some weeks, before returning to secure and well-stocked bases to recuperate. The advantage was defnitely with the Army—providing it had forceful leadership, and this it did.

General Sheridan organized a powerful task force of cavalry, infantry, and artillery augmented by four hundred regularly enrolled Indian Scouts from six different tribes. Its assignment was to find and destroy all hostile Sioux and Cheyenne camps.

After capturing two Sioux villages without resistance, the expedition came on the encampment of the band led by Morning Star (known to whites by his Sioux name, Dull Knife). It was tucked away in an enclosed mountain valley. Although the presence of the soldiers was known to the Cheyennes, the head chief of the Fox Military Society, Last Bull, who was an aberrant personality, forced the Cheyenne to stay in place, dancing all night—a death-defying madness. The attack came at dawn, and although the Cheyennes fought bravely, they were soundly defeated and their entire camp destroyed. The destitute survivors found refuge with the Sioux.

In the spring (1877), they voluntarily came in to Fort Keogh and surrendered. Thirty of the warriors enlisted in the United States Army as scouts.

The next year (1878), the Northern Cheyenne and Northern Arapaho signed a treaty with the United States in which they agreed to accept as a reservation some portion of the Southern Cheyenne-Arapaho reservation, or, as an alternative, a part of one of the Sioux reservations.

The Morning Star Outbreak: 1878   In Washington it was decided to consolidate all of the Cheyennes on the reservation on the Arkansas. Thus, following their surrender, one thousand Northern Cheyennes were moved under military escort to the Southern Cheyenne-Arapaho Reservation. There they camped through the summer of 1877, with little to do. They were reluctant residents and complained constantly and justly of the inadequacy of food issued to them. Dysentery, fevers, and despair sapped their energies. They were "homesick, heartsick, and sick in every way."

At last, one-third of the Northerners decided to defy the government. They would go back home, or die in the attempt. Led by Morning Star and Little Wolf, they departed in the dark of night. There were only eighty-five men to protect and escort two hundred and fifty women and children. The story has been well-told by George B. Grinnell (1915:383–398) and Maria Sandoz (1955). They fought and marched, fought and marched, eluding seventeen thousand troops sent to stop them.

After crossing the Platte, the fugitives split into two groups. That under Little Wolf shortly met Lieutenant W. P. Clark and some cavalry who were on the search for them. The Cheyennes surrendered peacefully, for they had won their goal. They were home. Little Wolf and his warriors enlisted in the United States Army to serve as scouts against the Sioux.

Morning Star and his small band of a hundred and fifty went west and eventually gave themselves up. For several months, they were held under favorable conditions at Fort Robinson, in western Nebraska, but the Cheyennes wished to be finally located at the Sioux Agency, called Red Cloud, in South Dakota. The administration in Washington stubbornly decided they should be returned to the Arkansas River reservation from which they had fled.

The Cheyennes adamantly refused. They were locked up in a barrack and given no food, water, or fuel for a week. Then they prepared to die. "It is true that we must die," they told each other. "But we will not die shut up here like dogs; we will die on the prairie; we will die fighting."

They dressed in their best, put together the five rifles and a dozen pistols which they had hidden on the women and children. Under a full moon, on a clear, cold January night, they broke through the windows of their barrack, and fled for the hills. Pursued by troops, they were unmercifully shot down—nearly half of them. Of the survivors, most were allowed to go to join the

Sioux at Pine Ridge. A few went south to the Southern Cheyenne-Arapaho reservation.

Cheyenne resistance was at an end. The tribe was henceforth to be under the control of the United States on terms set by it. The reservation period was about to begin for the Northerners, as it already had for the Southerners.

13 / The new era

An Indian reservation is an area of land "reserved" by treaty or executive order of the President of the United States for the use of one or more Indian tribes. Under law, the basic land is owned by the tribe, but is "held in trust" for the tribe by the government of the United States. Congress determines the fundamental guidelines for the administration of the trust. The ultimate responsibility for day-to-day and year-to-year administration rests with the President, as chief executive of the country. In practice, exercise of the President's power is delegated to the Secretary of the Interior, who in turn leaves all but major issues to the Commissioner of Indian Affairs. The Commissioner heads the Bureau of Indian Affairs, a unit within the Department of the Interior.

"Held in trust by the United States," when applied to Indian lands, has many specific meanings. At its heart, however, is the proposition that Indians at the outset were culturally unprepared to cope with the intricacies of getting along economically and politically in American society. Although the tribes had generally either sold or yielded most of their aboriginally held land under duress of conquest, the government assumed a moral responsibility for protecting the remaining tribal interests, according to its (the United States government's) lights.

In 1886, the United States Supreme Court clearly stated this fundamental idea in a landmark decision (*United States v. Kagama*) as follows:

> . . . These Indian tribes *are* the wards of the nation. They are communities *dependent* on the United States. Dependent largely for their daily food. Dependent for their political rights. They owe no allegiance to the States, and receive from them no protection. Because of the local ill feeling, the people of the States where they are found are often their deadliest enemies. From their very weakness and helplessness, so largely due to the course of dealing of the Federal Government with them, and the treaties in which it has been promised, there arises the duty of protection, and with it the power. This has always been recognized by the Executive and by Congress, and by this court, whenever the question has arisen (United States Reports 1886:118, 383–384).

What this means is that in the view of the federal government, until such time as the Indian tribes and individuals have acquired sufficient knowledge and economic power to be able to look after their own interests, the government will do it for them. The Great White Father in Washington thus became more than a romantic figure of speech.

Stripmining on the Northern Cheyenne reservation. (Courtesy Ken Kania)

RESERVATION DAYS FOR THE SOUTHERN CHEYENNE

At the end of the fighting, the buffalo were all but gone from the south and there were to be no more war parties. What were energetic Cheyenne males to do? As for the women, camp movements, which had taken up so much of their time in the past, were hardly possible within the confines of a reservation. Families had been decimated by death and disease. The Cheyennes had always had relatively few children, but the agency rolls for 1877 reveal startling figures: there were roughly seven hundred Cheyenne men and eleven hundred females (a sex ratio of 1 to 1.6). Of the children, there were only one thousand, or one for every one-and-a-half adults! All the Cheyennes on the reservation numbered less than three thousand, of whom nine hundred were Northern Cheyennes who had been forcibly removed from their homeland.

The task of the agent in charge of a reservation was first to keep the Indians from starving; next, to keep them calmed down; third, to protect them from the incursions of white cattlemen and other settlers upon their lands; and finally, to re-educate them toward a new way of life, called "civilizing the Indian."

To achieve the first task (warding off starvation), it was necessary to accept the fact that the Cheyennes would be wholly dependent on government hand-outs of beef, flour, bacon, and coffee until such time as they could grow enough crops or earn enough money to support themselves. The Cheyennes, like many other Indians, were put immediately on a system of public dole. The distribution of rations was erratic and never sufficient. It hardly sustained the body, and abject dependency corroded the spirit. Resentment led to many touchy incidents during the early years of reservation life, but the ever-ready availability of the force of the U.S. Army prevented unrest from exploding into serious outbreak.

Protection of the Southern Cheyennes in the security of their lands proved in the end to be beyond the powers of anyone in the Bureau of Indian Affairs or of the Cheyennes themselves. But first, a look at efforts toward "re-education."

For adults, the "civilizing" process meant constant exhortation and pressures from the reservation Agent and resident farmer to take to the plow and grow crops. This, in turn, meant that the Cheyennes had to be given work horses to replace the riding ponies they so highly prized. It also meant they had to buy, or be given, plows, cultivators, and wagons, and to be taught how to use them. But the sexist attitudes of the Cheyenne men held that gardening was women's work not suitable for warriors. It was a hard thing for a Cheyenne male to demean himself by turning his hand to the plow. Furthermore, the reservation was ill-suited to the small-scale farming techniques of the day. Those few Cheyenne who tried bravely to farm were greeted with crop failure more often than not. White men, wrote Agent Miles in 1881, who tried to grow corn and wheat in western Indian Territory would starve, even with all of their education and knowledge of farming. This was still true in the time of the Dust Bowl days of the 1930s.

It was not that the Cheyennes were against work, but they needed rewarding and ego-satisfying work. When they could get draught horses and wagons, they turned to hauling freight for the agency cross-country from the railroad at Wichita, Kansas. Soon there were more eager Cheyenne wagon owners than there were goods to be hauled. "The wagon then fell into disuse and the Indian returned to inactivity" (Berthrong 1976:68).

When warehouses were needed to store the goods brought into the agency, Cheyenne males were so eager to haul stone, burn lime, and turn a hand in raising the buildings, that they would labor without being on the payroll in hopes of getting paid after the fact. But the building boom, too, passed and another outlet of hope disappeared.

Agent Miles, struggling against misunderstanding opposition in Washington, soon perceived that where farming held little hope for the Southern Cheyennes, they might do very well as stock-raisers. The government did provide an experimental herd of cattle for the boys at the reservation school. In five years, it had increased from four hundred to over fifteen hundred head. Then the Commissioner of Indian Affairs, wanting to encourage rugged individualism, ordered the herd to be broken up and distributed among the Indian families. Three cows per family made no herd. They were soon eaten, traded, or gambled away. Support for a managed tribal herd would not be accepted as government policy, and the possibility of providing stock-raising as a new base of tribal livelihood was never tested—although the schoolboys had shown that it might just possibly have worked.

Re-education of the Cheyennes toward life in the world of the American had to be centered on the young. This was begun in 1877 with a group of young fighters who had been condemned for "war crimes" and sent as prisoners to Fort Marion (the old Spanish fortress) at St. Augustine, Florida. After a few years, some chose to go to Hampton Institute, a vocational school for blacks, in Virginia, and finally to the Carlisle Indian School, which was opened for them in Pennsylvania. Over the years, a number of Cheyenne boys and girls (especially the children of peace chiefs) went to Carlisle. During the summer months, they boarded out and worked in white households on farms and in towns in the East.

Others, in small numbers, were induced to attend mission and government-operated schools on the reservation. Quakers and Mennonites were the first to supply such service.

The goal of Indian education, as then provided, was to de-Indianize the new generations of the tribe by:

1. Collecting the children in boarding schools where they would be removed from the traditional influences of Indian camp life.
2. Cutting their hair and dressing them in American-style clothes.
3. Teaching them to speak, read, and write English, along with elementary arithmetic.
4. Training the boys in farming, blacksmithing, carpentry, butchering, shoe and harness repairing, and other useful crafts; teaching girls American cooking and baking, sewing, and other arts of housekeeping.
5. Teaching all the children the Gospel and the services of one or another of the Christian churches.

For the Cheyennes, Agent Miles put it succinctly: the return to the tribe of the school-trained young people would "kill much of the 'Indian' in the Indians of this agency in due time" (Berthrong 1976:85). Yet, for all the pressures[1] and despair that the Cheyenne were to endure in the hundred years that followed their conquest, the Cheyennes as a people never lost their identity or the last vestiges of their essential heritage.

The End of the Cheyenne-Arapaho Reservation   The Cheyenne-Arapaho reservation south of the Arkansas River was part of a large federal land block known as Indian Territory. Beginning in the 1830s, the United States had moved a number of southeastern tribes such as the Delaware, Cherokee, Chickasaw, Creeks, and Seminoles into it. The Territory had originally been conceived in the presidency of Andrew Jackson as a safe haven beyond the Mississippi where Indians would remain indefinitely out of the way of American settlement. Yet, within fifty years, expansionist-hungry settlers were clamoring for more, and yet more, of the territory for themselves.

When the buffalo were gone, in the mid-1880s, and the Cheyenne had failed as farmers and stock-raisers, the Bureau of Indian Affairs turned to leasing vast areas of grazing lands to white cattlemen as a means of getting cash income for the tribes and putting the unused land to productive use. The Cheyennes and Arapahos entered into an agreement engineered by the Department of the Interior to arrange five-to-ten year leases to whites at two cents per acre a year. What resulted was an incredible piece of political

---

[1] In 1903, for example, the Commissioner of Indian Affairs proposed to withhold the issue of food and clothing from Southern Cheyenne males who would not cut their hair.

boodling. Seven cattlemen obtained rights to use nearly four million of the four and a quarter million acres of the Cheyenne-Arapaho reserve. This gave them use of ninety percent of the land belonging to the two tribes—more than a hundred thousand square miles!

By 1885, the ranges were stocked with nearly a quarter million head of cattle.

The lease system, however, was doomed to early failure. Members of the Dog Soldier band, who were now crowded into the small remaining living area with the rest of the Cheyennes, took over as the dominant power within the tribe. They could act as an organized body to terrorize other Cheyennes who tried to farm or run small herds of their own. They boldly killed such cattle of the leasees as they wished and burned the grass on the ranges. They adamantly kept their own children out of the schools. They expressed contempt for the authority of the agent and the power of the small military garrisons at the closest army posts.

The government response was to replace the civilian agent with a military man. The army garrisons were reinforced and President Cleveland summarily cancelled the cattle leases, giving the barons forty days to remove all their herds from the reservation.

The Cheyennes were now back where they were before, but without the cash from lease money.

The Break-up of the Reservation   In 1887, Congress decided that the way to encourage Indian progress toward assimilation into American society was to make it possible for them to become citizens in their own right. It passed the Dawes Severalty Act, which provided that each Indian man, woman, and child could be allotted a plot of land in individual ownership. There was a "Catch Twenty-five" to the ownership, however. The land would not be sold for twenty-five years, but would remain in trust administered by the government. After twenty-five years, the allottee would receive a fee-simple title (that is, outright ownership) to his (or her) land. The Indian owner who had left the tribe, would then become "competent," a citizen of the United States subject to the laws of the state in which he or she resided, and free to keep, rent, sell, or give away the property, according to personal desire. All leftover reservation land could then be bought by the federal government for future disposition.

As for the Southern Cheyennes, the government lost little time in putting the Dawes Act into effect.

When the assignment of individual allotments was completed in the spring of 1892, a little over 500,000 acres remained in Cheyenne and Arapaho hands. The remaining 3,500,000 acres of their reservation were bought by the government for homesteading by whites.

The Cheyenne-Arapaho Reservation ceased to exist, and the Southern Cheyenne had lost their tribal land base forever.

The Northern Cheyenne Reservation   When the wars were over, fate treated the Northern Cheyenne bands somewhat better than it did the Southerners. Most of the Northern bands came to Fort Keogh after their surrender, and stayed there for several years. Finally, they moved west to the Tongue River, in Montana, to settle in a beautiful country of their own choosing. In 1884, the President, by executive order, set aside 371,200 acres of surrounding land as their reservation. This was enlarged to 460,000 acres in 1900 and today includes 440,000 acres.

There were virtually no white settlers in the Tongue River area in the 1880s. The land lay along no migration routes and remained physically isolated until the 1950s, when the first paved highway through the reservation was laid. Although there have been white cattle ranches in and around the Tongue River Reservation for half a century, the Northern Cheyennes have not been subject to the kind of settler's land-lust which stripped the Cheyenne and Arapaho of their tribal holdings.

Individual land allotments were not made among the Northern Cheyenne until 1926—and more importantly, the unallotted lands were not opened to white homesteading. Mineral rights under allotted lands were reserved for the benefit of the tribe for fifty years.

Today the three thousand Northern Cheyennes own approximately 270,000 acres of tribal land in common, while about 164,000 acres are allotted, and the government holds almost 7,000 acres for its own use in connection with the agency administration. Since 1954, the Northern Cheyenne Tribal Council, first on its own initiative, and later with government assistance, has been buying back such allotted lands as go up for sale. So it has been gradually increasing the tribal land holdings and the community has a solid base on which to exist.

RELIGIOUS SURVIVAL

Hard as the Cheyenne struggled to survive on government annuities and the meager monies they received from the lease of their lands during the first sixty years or more after their defeat, the fight to retain their Cheyenneness through their religion meant even more to them.

We have seen how the Great Ceremonies expressed the embodiment of the tribal soul and well-being in the ritual of the Medicine Arrows Renewal, and how the world was revitalized each spring in the ceremonial act of the Sun Dance. The Massaum (Crazy Animal Dance) was essentially a hunting society ritual, and now that the Cheyennes were no longer hunters, they were willing enough to let the Massaum ritual go.

The Sun Dance was something else, however. Not only do the Cheyennes need its renewing beneficence; the whole universe does, according to the deepest Cheyenne belief. Likewise, the maintenance of the Medicine Arrows is a sacred obligation of the Cheyennes to themselves, the holiest sacrament of the Cheyennes as a People.

Early Indian Bureau agents did not understand these things. They simply viewed the ceremonies as uncivilized and barbarous (especially the acts of self-torture and the ritual intercourse between priests and the wives of pledgers). Even the more religiously tolerant agents objected to the continuation of the ceremonies because they took the Cheyennes away from their farms at the most critical time of the planting season. In the case of the Southern Cheyennes, the agents also wanted to reduce the power of the Dog Soldiers, who were destroying the fences and killing the horses of those Cheyennes who wanted to stay away from the ceremonies to tend their farms and crops.

The Ghost Dance Movement   Suppression of the Sun Dance was not too difficult in the early 1890s. A new religious movement, known as the Ghost Dance, had sprung up among the Paiute Indians of Nevada and had spread eastward to the Plains tribes. The Ghost Dance is a classic example of a *na-*

tivistic movement in times of *cultural crisis.* Such movements aim to reconstitute a destroyed but not forgotten way of life. This one was also Messianic. It was founded by a partly Christianized Paiute who, in a state of trance, went to heaven and was instructed by God. Heaven was full of all the Indians who had died. They were young once more, happy and vigorous, enjoying games and dances, living well amidst inexhaustible supplies of game.

God told Wovoka, the Paiute, to return to earth and preach peace and love to his people: they should not lie, steal, quarrel among themselves, or fight against the whites. But if they worked hard and danced as God instructed, then the land would be transformed as it appeared in heaven and people would live in happy harmony with their dead loved ones forever immortal.

The Paiute Messiah's message spread like wildfire to the despairing tribes across the plains, transforming the doctrine as it spread from tribe to tribe. However, one central theme remained unaltered. The dead would be restored, the buffalo and antelope would return in numbers, the land would be eternally green, and all Indians would live healthily, happily in the old way. The Ghost Dance would hasten the arrival of this day.

In the fall of 1889, a Northern Cheyenne made a pilgrimage to get firsthand information from the Messiah. He returned to Montana in the early spring (1890) bearing the message of the Christ (Wovoka). The report, according to James Mooney, "caused the wildest excitement among the Cheyenne, and after several long debates on the subject, the Ghost Dance was inaugurated at the several camps" (Mooney 1896:819). The Ghost Dance, it had been decided, was a better way to carry out the world renewal functions of the Sun Dance, and so it was voluntarily substituted for the latter.

The Southern Cheyenne took up the movement more slowly, but they also sent their delegates to Nevada, and by 1893 the Ghost Dance in various forms had displaced most of the other Southern Cheyenne ceremonies.

By the end of the decade, however, the promise of the Ghost Dance had not been fulfilled. The Cheyennes returned to their ancient ceremonies and to a new religious form which did not hold out so much promise but which nonetheless held familiar appeal.

The Peyote Cult   Peyote is a small, grey-green spineless cactus (*Lophophora williamsii*) native to Mexico and parts of Texas. It contains a number of alkaloids capable of producing a variety of physiological effects on human beings when eaten or taken as "tea." In a proper ritual context, it produces color transformations and auditory and visual hallucinations—visions. It is not a narcotic and does not produce chemical dependency.

The ritual use of peyote goes back to pre-Columbian Mexico. The Spanish *conquistadores* found it in religious contexts in central Mexico, and its ritual use flourishes today among certain of the mountain peoples of Mexico.

The name "peyote" is derived from the Aztec word for caterpillar, *peyotl,* because the white fuzzy top of the peyote plant looks like the back of a caterpillar.

The ritual use of peyote was introduced into the southern plains by the Apache nearly three hundred years ago. The Cheyennes, however, did not take it up until about the same time as the Ghost Dance.

The Peyote Cult developed essentially as a group experience, although some people eat peyote alone. A ceremony usually lasts all night. Among the Cheyenne, it is ordinarily held in a tipi, although not necessarily so. Wor-

Medicine, Blackwolf, and Little Chief. Three leaders in a Northern Cheyenne peyote ceremony. Photo by E. A. Hoebel, 1937.

shippers sit around the inside wall of the tipi. In the center is an altar shaped of earth in the form of a crescent moon. Between the horns of the moon a small fire is kept burning throughout the night. Prayers, a mixture of appeals to the Maiyun, to God, Jesus, and the Bible are interspersed between the songs and drumming. Dried heads of the peyote plants are eaten and visions are experienced. Some suppliants take advantage of the occasional pauses to tell the group of the content of their visions, and the head priest comments on what has been revealed.

The great appeal of the peyote ritual is that it brings people together in a serious social setting which provides intimate reinforcement for the struggling individual. It is basically Indian—especially in its virtual guarantee of vision experiences, in its drumming and singing, and in its setting in the tipi. At the same time, it clearly signals a break with the past (in contrast to the Ghost Dance), in that it is recognized as a new religion given by God to the Indians in their time of greatest need. Hence, the inclusion of specific Christian elements in the ritual performances. The eating of the peyote is interpreted as a sacrament.

Strenuous efforts by the Cheyenne-Arapaho Agent to have the Peyote Cult legally outlawed in 1907 failed. Ten years later, the leaders of peyote groups among the Southern Cheyenne, Kiowa, Comanche, Ponca, and Osage tribes were able to incorporate the religion as a recognized church under the laws of the State of Oklahoma. Known as The Native American Church, its chief function is to insure the constitutional guarantee of freedom of religious worship to its membership.

Missionary efforts have been continuous among the Cheyennes for nearly a hundred years, but only a relatively small number are today committed Christians. Fully eighty percent of the adult Northern Cheyennes are members of the Native American Church.

Although Peyoteists may participate in the Sun Dance, there is a strong feeling that special priests, such as the Arrow and Medicine Hat Keepers and traditional priests of other ceremonies, ought not to be Peyoteists. Peyoteism represents a new native religion which replaces the old.

The Sun Dance and Arrow Renewal Today   All efforts through the first quarter of this century to eradicate the Sun Dance of the Cheyennes failed. Finally, after 1926, the Bureau of Indian Affairs officially recognized the right of all Indians to express their religious beliefs.

Early in the century, the Cheyennes had shifted the date for holding their Sun Dances from sometime in June to the Fourth of July. This was to accommodate their agents' insistence that the dance not be held until after their crops were safely planted and their children were home from school. Today, the performance of the Sun Dance at the time of the Fourth links the Cheyenne annual world revitalization to the celebration of the birth of the nation. Approaching the Northern Cheyenne Sun Dance site, a visitor confronts a handlettered sign, "Quiet Please. No Fireworks Allowed. Religious Ceremony in Progress."

Although many details of the Sun Dance and Arrow Renewal Rites have been lost to the Cheyennes, enough remains in memory and in a couple of handbooks written in 1939, when surviving priests took some of the "best young men" into the mountains for two weeks "to teach them the mysteries" so that the ceremonies should not die out. The vitality of both ceremonies is well attested in Father Peter J. Powell's intimate accounts and photographs in the two-volume work published in 1969 (*Sweet Medicine: The Continuing Role of the Sacred Arrows, the Sun Dance, and the Sacred Buffalo Hat in Northern Cheyenne History*).

The Sun Dance is actually the more flourishing ritual and is performed separately by both the Southern and Northern Cheyennes. The Medicine Arrows, although they have been taken north to Montana in recent years, normally reside with the Southern Cheyenne. Renewal ceremonies are held less frequently in fulfillment of personal vows.

In the heyday of Cheyenne culture, attendance at an Arrow Ceremony, it will be remembered, was compulsory for *all* Cheyennes—except murderers and their close kinsmen (p. 56). Today, participation seems to attract the interest of only a few persons. The Arrow Ceremony held in July of 1968 brought together only twenty tents of Southern Cheyennes, plus a delegation from Montana of two representatives of the Northern Cheyennes. The Northern Cheyenne Tribal Council made an appropriation toward the purchase of food and offerings for the ceremony—and transmitted the sum via Western Union.

The Arrow Keeper in 1962, in the traditionalist way, wished his people would care more about their religion and lamented the way the younger Cheyenne tend to "mess themselves up" with drinking, fights, auto accidents, and occasional murder (Ottaway 1969:12).

The Medicine Hat is still revered and still has its official Keeper in Montana. The bundle in which it is wrapped is displayed outside the Hat Keeper's tipi at the Sun Dance, but the rituals associated with the Hat have been lost and are no longer performed.

MODERN POLITICAL AND SOCIAL ACTION

The old formal council of Chiefs has long been gone. The last ritual renewal of Chiefs among the Northern Cheyenne took place in 1892. By 1935, all but two had died, and had not been replaced. There were band leaders, in both the North and South, as there had been in the old days. These are the men who rose to positions of recognized leadership among the several camp groups in the early days of reservation life or among the neighborhood families of a kindred after the time of land allotments. They are looked on as chiefs, and meeting to discuss tribal problems, they became recognized as a Society of Chiefs—not a true Tribal Council, because the sacred chief's rituals have not been passed on.

Some of the military societies became extinct after the conquest of the Cheyennes, but among the Northern Cheyennes the Elk, Crazy Dogs, and Fox continued as vital organizations. Up until 1900, they worked to prevent cattle stealing and to arrest troublemakers. For a while, the Fox Soldiers made a group enterprise out of plowing, with the encouragement of their agent. Just as on the tribal buffalo hunts of by-gone days, the whole society "attacked" an Indian farmer's land and with a half-a-dozen or more plows at once and soon had it prepared for planting. Then they would move as a body on to the next farm. One year, the Foxes announced that any member who failed to show up for plowing would be whipped. When Medicine Bull stayed home to mend his fences, the Foxes rode down to his place, firing their guns and quirting him (cf., page 58, above). Then they made him get on his horse and go plowing right away.

Among the Southern Cheyennes, the truculent resistance and arrogance of the Dog Soldiers helped to bring the Indian Bureau to a policy decision not to encourage the activities of the military societies, but to put the law enforcement needs of the reservations in the hands of a uniformed police force and appointed Indian judges. This program was introduced among most tribes in the late 1880s.

After allotment and the admission of Oklahoma into the Union as a state in 1906, the Southern Cheyenne came under the jurisdiction of the state law enforcement agencies, as any other citizens. The Northern Cheyenne, on the other hand, have legal jurisdiction over tribal members living on the reservation (except for certain major crimes, such as homicide, burglary, robbery, arson, and rape, which have been made federal offenses), and the tribal police are employees of the tribe. On the personal level, there is today so much lack of self-control that the police have a most unenviable job trying to cope with public drunkenness, fights, automobile accidents and traffic violations. In 1967 and 1968 the Northern Cheyenne tribal police made 2,322 and 2,671 arrests for misdemeanors. The police in turn are subject to such political and community pressures that few of them stay on the job for long. There has been no adequate substitute found for the military societies as guardians of law and order.

What the soldier societies do is to look after the Sun Dance, select the Keepers of the Medicine Arrows and Sacred Buffalo Hat, and participate in decisions affecting them. They work closely with the Society of Chiefs and the Medicine Keepers in an effort to keep the spiritual and religious system of the Cheyennes alive and functioning. In this endeavor, society members from both the Northern and Southern Cheyennes have taken up the practice of making religious pilgrimages to the cave in the Sacred Mountain in South Dakota, for instruction from Maiyun. It was begun during World War II in an effort to help win the war and has become more and more frequent in recent years.

The New Deal for Indians   The administration of Franklin Delano Roosevelt ushered in a new era in the federal administration of Indian affairs, as it did in many other aspects of government. The Indian Reorganization Act was passed in 1934. It put a stop to all further allotment of Indian lands and returned to tribal ownership all reservation lands previously declared surplus. It also provided for the use of federal funds to repurchase lands in order to consolidate reservation land blocks. For the Northern Cheyenne, who had had their first individual land allotments only eight years previously, this assured the survival of their land base indefinitely—in contrast to what had happened to the Southern Cheyenne.

The Indian Reorganization Act also provided for a modernized form of tribal government for those tribes that wished to choose it. The tribe could be chartered as a corporation by the United States. The corporation would operate under a written constitution, would have a tribally elected Council (Board of Directors), a Chairman of the Council, and other officers. The Council would be endowed with powers of borrowing money for development projects from federal or private sources, and of enacting laws within the jurisdiction of the tribe. The aim of the Act was to limit the absolutism of the Bureau of Indian Affairs by involving the Indians in an increasing exercise of self-government. Strenuous efforts were also made to upgrade the quality of education for Indian youth and to encourage expression of Indian self-identity through what remained or could be recovered of tribal crafts and ceremonialism. Health services were also considerably improved.

The Southern Cheyenne and Arapaho incorporated as a single body with a Council of seven Cheyennes and seven Arapahos.

The Northern Cheyenne also elected to take advantage of the Act. Generally speaking, the Tribal Business Committee (as the Corporation Council is usually called) are the better-educated, part Cheyenne-part white members of the tribe who are not strongly traditionally oriented. The Northern Cheyenne, in particular, have had effective leadership in the years since World War II. In the 1950s and 1960s, under John Woodenlegs, they entered into a privately-sponsored program assisted by the American Association on Indian Affairs. This program enlisted the assistance of interested Montanans to work with the tribal officers in nonbureaucratic technical assistance. It enabled the tribe to bid competitively for the reacquisition of all allotted Indian lands which came up for sale, to start its own tribal herd, a tourist information center, crafts shop, and a program to induce small manufacturing businesses to establish plants on the reservation. The Northern Cheyenne tribal goal is the repurchase of *all* allotted land over a period of fifty years.

Meanwhile, in 1947, Congress passed the Indian Claims Act. This enabled all Indian tribes to sue for recovery of value on all lands which had been illegally taken from them without a valid treaty agreement, or for which the payment had been unconscionably low. In 1961, the Court of Indian Claims held that the $1,162,000 which the Northern Cheyenne and Arapaho had received for their interest in all Cheyenne-Arapaho lands *was* unconscionably low when set against a fair market value in 1865 of $23,500,000 for the lands as a whole. It recommended that the Northern Cheyenne and Arapaho be paid $10,588,000 by Congress. Of this, the Northern Cheyenne received one-half in 1963. The Southern Cheyenne-Arapaho tribe received slightly more than ten million for their half of the lost lands.

Arrangements were made for limited cash payments to tribal members from the awards, but the rest is held as a capital fund for developmental projects, student loans, and so on.

SOCIOECONOMIC NEEDS AND POTENTIAL

The social and economic plight of the Southern Cheyenne is disheartening. Few of the Cheyennes themselves work what remains of their farm lands, nor do they live on the land. Most are located in ethnic neighborhoods in western Oklahoma small towns. They live on lease and welfare money which averages around $1,000 a year per family in an area where the average income for white families is close to $15,000 a year (Schlesier 1974:278). The unemployment rate was over eighty percent in 1972 at a time when a national unemployment rate of seven percent was considered to be a near calamity.

In contrast to the Northern Cheyenne situation, the Southern Cheyenne-Arapaho combined land base is steadily evaporating. In 1967, there were just a little over one hundred thousand allotted acres still in Indian hands. In three years (1967–70), nine thousand acres went on the auction block, reducing the residue to well under a hundred thousand acres.

In spite of their close affinity and frequency of intermarriage, the Cheyennes and Arapahos do not form an organic social and political group—even though the United States has said they are a united entity ever since the time of the Fort Laramie Treaty in 1851. The Cheyenne-Arapaho Tribal Business Committee has a hard time pulling together for constructive common action. And among the Southern Cheyenne, the contest between the pariah, but powerful, Dog Soldiers band and the traditional bands led by Peace Chiefs has further hindered constructive common action.

To overcome their ennervating state of social and political paralysis the Southern Cheyenne in 1972, under the aegis of the Medicine Arrow Keeper, set up their own independent structure in most modern terms: a chartered corporation to be known as the Southern Cheyenne Research and Human Development Association, Inc., a counterpart to the Northern Cheyenne Research and Human Development Association. May it serve its people well!

The Northern Cheyenne were, until after World War II, looked upon by many outsiders as "conservative." It is true that in their isolation, and due to "benign neglect" by the Bureau of Indian Affairs, they retained much of their identity and sense of self-worth and dignity. The Northern Cheyennes of the 1930s were poor—but proud. There was little alcoholism or serious social despair.

World War II and expanding experience with the outer world produced two contrasting effects. Some returning veterans dedicated themselves to leadership and social action. Others could neither accept the constraints of the limited cultural environment of the reservation nor surmount the loneliness of the cut-off Cheyenne who chose to go into the cities. These returned to the Tongue River Reservation, but they drowned their despair in drink or suicide, giving the Cheyenne population in the 1950s and 1960s one of the highest suicide rates in the nation. The tradition of suicide, always strong in Cheyenne culture, was formerly achieved for men through the glorious death sought in battle. Only women actually killed themselves.

Still, the core of leadership among the Northerners held firm, motivated by a spirit of practicality and forward-looking vision. It was most eloquently expressed by the tribal chairman, Mr. John Woodenlegs, at the 1963 annual meeting of the American Association on Indian Affairs in New York. He said, in part:

> The Morning Star has always been a special star to the Cheyennes ever since anyone can remember. It lights the morning sky and shines more brightly than other stars. It has a different color . . .
>
> It has its own name in our language—*Wo-He-Hiv* . . .
>
> We fought on the Little Big Horn, the Custer Battle, to keep some of our land. Now to use this land we have a cattle program, a tribal herd, and we have about two thousand five hundred yearling steers running around out there now. On the range we can truthfully say that this is Indian cattle and not leased range or someone else's cattle.
>
> We found a design to use as a trademark for our trible. It's the Morning Star symbol and the Cheyennes used it when they had the ceremony at Sun Dances. They used to paint it on their bodies as a guide. . . . So the Tribal Council when they wanted a trademark . . . now . . . use this. We put it on the cattle too— it's a good tribal brand and the Cheyenne are using it now. . . .
>
> We are also asking for on-the-job training [for our people]. We want some plumbers and carpenters and electricians, and we also want a public high school [in the center of the reservation]. . . .
>
> I would like the Indians to keep up . . . where Indians could be lawyers and doctors, maybe bankers, airline pilots, or maybe even a moon affair, a man that's going to the moon.
>
> We'd like to catch up that way. . . .
>
> We hope and pray that we keep on going, and to keep our land we are using this star, this Morning Star. It has been our guiding light. It will give us life in our hearts and will guide us in the days to come (Woodenlegs 1963:3).

The Northern Cheyenne today call themselves The Morning Star People.

Coal in the North   The Morning Star People have kept their land. Now, in the 1970s, and for the rest of the present century, they are confronted with a wholly new problem. They sit on a vast energy resource. Virtually the entire reservation overlies easily accessible lignite (very soft brown coal), five billion tons of it, which has suddenly become highly desired for generation of electric power in the midst of the national energy crisis.

Coal and power companies are champing to build coal gasification plants and to obtain lease rights to strip the surface lands and extract the underlying coal. One company, in 1972, offered to build the Northern Cheyennes a $1.5 million health center and to pay them an estimated $7.5 million in royalties, plus an approximate $2.5 million cash bonus for coal lease rights to seventy thousand acres, or 16 percent of the reservation.

The Department of the Interior, with the consent of the Tribal Council, had already arranged much less favorable terms for extraction leases on smaller areas.

The Northern Cheyennes decided to take another look at the whole question: How much land, if any, should they sacrifice to stripping, by whom, for how much, and under what specific conditions? Tens of millions of potential dollars are at stake for a tribal population of two thousand six hundred, mostly poor, people. Do they want to sacrifice their beautiful and isolated rangelands for material prosperity in the midst of mining towns and the new settlers who will be coming in, not to farm or run cattle but to operate huge electric power and coal gasification plants?

In 1974, the Northern Cheyenne Tribal Council voted to demand that the Secretary of the Interior terminate and cancel all existing coal exploration permits and leases on the grounds that 1) the companies were willfully violating the established lease terms; but more importantly 2) that the leasing procedures used by the Department of the Interior violated the provisions of the National Environmental Policy Act of 1969 and the Code of Federal Regulations. The Secretary of the Interior acquiesced in some respects. A big legal battle is on, for the stakes are high.

It is possible that the Northern Cheyenne will do their own mining of the coal and move into petrochemical manufacturing through a diverse number of industries. If this is the route they follow, they can do the least possible environmental damage to their beautiful country while spreading the economic benefits of their enterprise well into the next century.

The Morning Star People may or may not become the Arabs of America. Yet, in terms of what they have already done successfully to challenge the shabby policies of the Department of the Interior in its trusteeship over Indian lands, and in terms of what they may yet achieve on their own behalf in the wise exercise of self-determination in the use of their land, they have deservedly won the environmentalist's encomium; to wit:

> It is a strange commentary, but the Northern Cheyenne Indians are at this moment the most important tribe to America. What has been done to them—and the nature of their response—bids fair to affect not only all Indians but a very large number of whites (Toole 1976:49).

As for the coal—"It will either save us or be our ruination. The hell of it is, we don't know which way it will go" (Ibid.: 68).

Bibliography

Anderson, R., 1956. The Buffalo Men, A Cheyenne Ceremony of Petition Deriving from the Sutaio. *Southwestern Journal of Anthropology*, Vol. 12, pp. 92–104.

Bennett, J. W., 1944. The Development of Ethnological Theories as Illustrated by the Plains Indian Sun Dance. *American Anthropologist*, Vol. 46, pp. 162–181.

Berthrong, D. J., 1963. *The Southern Cheyennes*. Norman, Okla.: University of Oklahoma Press.

———, 1976. *The Cheyenne and Arapaho Ordeal: Reservation and Agency Life in the Indian Territory, 1875–1907*. Norman, Okla.: University of Oklahoma Press.

Coues, E. (ed.), 1897. *New Light on the Early History of the Greater Northwest: The Manuscript Journals of Alexander Henry and of David Thompson, 1799–1814*. New York: F. P. Harper.

Dorsey, G. A., 1905. The Cheyenne. *Field Columbia Museum Anthropological Series*, Vol. IX, Nos. 1 and 2.

Eastman, E. G., 1935. *Pratt: The Red Man's Moses*. Norman, Okla.: University of Oklahoma Press.

Eggan, F., 1955. The Cheyenne and Arapaho Kinship System. In *Social Anthropology of North American Tribes* (enlarged edition). Chicago: University of Chicago Press, pp. 35–95.

Fortune, R. F., 1932. *Sorcerers of Dobu: The Social Anthropology of the Dobu Islanders of the Western Pacific*. New York: Dutton.

Gladwin, T., 1957. Personality Structure in the Plains. *Anthropological Quarterly*, Vol. 30, pp. 111–124.

Grinnell, G. B., 1915. *The Fighting Cheyennes*. New York: Scribner.

———, 1923. *The Cheyenne Indians: Their History and Ways of Life*. New Haven: Yale University Press.

Hafen, L. R., 1974. Historical Background and Development of the Arapaho-Cheyenne Land Area. In D. L. Horr (ed.), *Arapaho-Cheyenne Indians*. New York: Garland Publishing Co., pp. 97–225.

Hoebel, E. A., n.d. Cheyenne Field Notes. Unpublished.

Jablow, J., 1950. The Cheyenne in Plains Indian Trade Relations, 1795–1840. *American Ethnological Society Monograph XIX*.

Kluckhohn, C., 1949. The Philosophy of the Navaho Indians. In F. S. C. Northrop (ed.), *Ideological Differences and World Order*. New Haven: Yale University Press, pp. 356–384.

Lavender, D., 1954. *Bent's Fort*. Garden City, N.Y.: Doubleday.

Lewis, O., 1942. The Effects of White Contact Upon Blackfoot Culture with Special Reference to the Role of the Fur Trade. *American Ethnological Society Monograph VI*.

Llewellyn, K. N., and Hoebel, E. A., 1941. *The Cheyenne Way: Conflict and Case Law in Primitive Jurisprudence*. Norman, Okla.: University of Oklahoma Press.

Lowie, R. H., 1924. *Primitive Religion*. New York: Boni and Liveright.

———, 1935. *The Crow Indians*. New York: Farrar and Rinehart.

Michelson, T., 1932. The Narrative of a Southern Cheyenne Woman. *Smithsonian Miscellaneous Collections,* Vol. 87, No. 5.

Mooney, J., 1896. The Ghost Dance Religion and the Sioux Outbreak of 1890. *Bureau of American Ethnology, Annual Reports,* No. 14, Part 2.

————, 1907. The Cheyenne Indians. *American Anthropological Association Memoirs,* Vol. 1, Part 6.

Ottaway, H. N., 1969. *The Cheyenne Arrow Ceremony, 1968.* Wichita, Kans: Department of Anthropology, Kansas State University.

Petter, R. C., 1907. Sketch of the Cheyenne Grammar. *American Anthropological Association Memoirs,* Vol. 1, Part 6.

————, 1915. *English-Cheyenne Dictionary.* Kettle Falls, Wash.

————, 1952. *Cheyenne Grammar.* Newton, Kans.: Mennonite Publication Office.

Pettitt, G. A., 1946. Primitive Education in North America. *University of California Publications in American Archaeology and Ethnology,* Vol. 43, No. 1.

Powell, P. J., 1969. *Sweet Medicine: The Continuing Role of the Sacred Arrows, the Sun Dance, and the Sacred Buffalo Hat in Northern Cheyenne History.* Norman, Okla.: University of Oklahoma Press.

Sandoz, M., 1955. *Cheyenne Autumn.* New York: McGraw-Hill.

Schlesier, K. N., 1974. Action Anthropology and the Southern Cheyenne. *Anthropology Today,* Vol. 15, pp. 277–283.

Stands in Timber, J., and Liberty, M. (with assistance of R. M. Utley), 1967. *Cheyenne Memories.* New Haven: Yale University Press.

Toole, R. K., 1976. *The Rape of the Great Plains.* Boston: Little, Brown.

Tyrrell, J. B. (ed.), 1916. *David Thompson's Narratives of His Explorations in Western America, 1784–1812.* Toronto: The Champlain Society.

Underhill, R. M., 1948. Ceremonial Patterns in the Greater Southwest. *American Ethnological Society Monograph XII.*

United States Reports, 1886. *United States v. Kagama,* pp. 383–384.

Ward, R. D., 1925. *The Climates of the United States.* Boston: Ginn.

Webb, W. P., 1931. *The Great Plains.* Boston: Ginn.

Wilson, G. R., 1934. The Hidatsa Earth-lodge. *American Museum of Natural History Anthropological Papers,* Vol. 33.

Woodenlegs, J., 1963. Morning Star, 1963. *Indian Affairs,* No. 51, p. 3.

Recommended reading

ADDITIONAL BOOKS ON THE CHEYENNE AND THE PLAINS INDIANS

Densmore, F., 1936. Cheyenne and Arapaho Music. *Southwest Museum Papers,* No. 10, pp. 9–111.
> For the music specialist.
Grinnell, G. B., 1926, 1962. *By Cheyenne Campfires.* New Haven: Yale University Press.
> A highly readable collection of Cheyenne war stories, legends, and sacred myths.
———, 1920. *When the Buffalo Ran.* New Haven: Yale University Press.
> A delightful biography of a Cheyenne's boyhood.
Lowie, R. H., 1963. *Indians of the Plains.* Garden City, N.Y.: Natural History Press.
> The one basic book on the Indian cultures of the Plains area in the English language.
Mails, T. E., 1972. *The Mystic Warriors of the Plains.* Garden City, N.Y.: Doubleday.
> Valuable for its illustrations only. The text is uneven and fragmentary.
Marquis, T. B., 1957. *Wooden Leg: A Warrior Who Fought Custer.* Lincoln, Nebr.: University of Nebraska Press.
> An authentic and interesting autobiography of a Northern Cheyenne.
Oliver, S. C., 1962. Ecology and Cultural Continuity as Contributing Factors in the Social Organization of Plains Indians. *University of California Publications in American Archaeology and Ethnology,* Vol. 48, pp. 1–90.
> Excellent comparative tribal summaries and scholarly overview of the interplay of differing historical and cultural backgrounds in relation to subsistence modes and adaptation to the Plains environment.
Petersen, K. D., 1968. *Howling Wolf: A Cheyenne Warrior's Graphic Interpretation of His People.* Palo Alto, Calif.: American West Publishing Co.
> Fascinating paintings and drawings by a pacified Cheyenne warrior, plus valuable commentary.
Secoy, F. R., 1953. Changing Military Patterns on the Great Plains (17th Century through Early 19th Century). *American Ethnological Society Monograph XXI.*
> An ethnohistorical account of the effects of the successive introduction of the horse and the gun on warfare among the Plains Indians.
Seger, J. H. (S. Vestal, ed.), 1924. *Early Days Among the Cheyenne and Arapaho Indians.* Norman, Okla.: University of Oklahoma Press.
> A simple and straightforward story of the Cheyennes in the early reservation days, told by a brave and understanding agency employee.
Wedel, W. R., 1961. *Prehistoric Man on the Great Plains.* Norman, Okla.: University of Oklahoma Press.
> The authoritative archaeological synthesis of the development of Plains Indian cultures from late Glacial to proto-historic times.
Wood, W. R., 1971. Biesterfeldt: A Post-Contact Coalescent Site on the Northeastern Plains. *Smithsonian Contributions to Anthropology,* No. 15.

Pages 51–71 provide the best analysis of archaeological and historical evidence of the Cheyenne move from the Mississippi to the Missouri River.

SPECIAL BIBLIOGRAPHIES

Hoebel, E. A., 1977. *The Plains Indians: A Critical Bibliography.* Bloomington, Ind.: Indiana University Press.
This selected bibliography introduces two hundred of the most useful books on Plains Indians and their culture histories set in a narrative essay.
Murdock, G. P., and O'Leary, T. J., 1975. *Ethnographic Bibliography of North America,* 4th ed. *Volume 5: Plains and Southwest.* New Haven: Human Relations Area Files Press.
An unannotated bibliography listing five thousand publications on Plains Indians. Pages 62–69 list two hundred and forty books and articles on the Cheyenne. This work is an invaluable aid to research.